Waters Swift and Still

Edited by CRAIG WOODS
and DAVID SEYBOLD

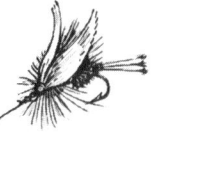

Waters Swift and Still

Foreword by Gary LaFontaine

Illustrated by Robert Seaman

WINCHESTER PRESS/Tulsa, Oklahoma

Copyright © 1982 by
Craig Woods and David Seybold

ALL RIGHTS RESERVED

Library of Congress Cataloging in Publication Data
Main entry under title:
Waters swift and still.
  1. Fly fishing. 2. Fishing. I. Woods, Craig.
II. Seybold, David.
SH456.W336   799.1'2   82-1840
ISBN 0-87691-357-5   AACR2

Published by *Winchester Press*
1421 South Sheridan Road
P.O. Box 1260
Tulsa, Oklahoma 74101

Book design by Design for Publishing
Printed in United States of America

1 2 3 4 5   86 85 84 83 82

For Nick Lyons,
whose enthusiasm for angling
and commitment to publishing
have touched this and
so many other books about fly-fishing.

Acknowledgments

The editors would like to thank the following individuals for their help in making this book a reality:
Nick Lyons,
Norma Carter,
and Don Poulson.

Contents

Foreword *by Gary LaFontaine,* 11
Prologue *by Craig Woods,* 17
The Way of Consolation *by Art Lee,* 21
Gamboling at Frenchman's *by Robert Traver,* 37
Some Reflections on Failure *by Ernest Schwiebert,* 53
Catch and Release and Other Things *by Nelson Bryant,* 69
Notes on Alaska *by John Randolph,* 79
City Angler *by Nick Lyons,* 97
Home Waters *by Charles Gaines,* 109
Fly-Fishing: An Angler's Perspective *by Lee Wulff,* 121
Stillwaters Run Deep *by John Merwin,* 137
October: A Northwest Idyll *by Steve Raymond,* 149
Just a Rod Away *by Geoffrey Norman,* 161
The Bonefish Flats *by Charles F. Waterman,* 173
Epilogue *by David Seybold,* 189
About the Authors, 193

Foreword
Gary LaFontaine

M Y STUDY of fly-fishing literature, both old and new, has been particularly extensive lately. During the preparation of a book on the history of the literature, it has been impossible for me to avoid comparing different eras. My conclusion is that the best writing is no better and the worst writing is no worse now than the highs and lows have ever been, but that overall the average quality of fly-fishing literature is probably better now than ever before in this country.

Fishing writing can be broken down roughly into three categories—where-to, how-to, and why-to. It can be argued that how-to and where-to are but two facets of a single genre of instructional writing. The point is that both categories are chiefly concerned with conveying information, instruction of some kind, whereas a piece of mood writing is centered on philosophical or esthetic concerns or on the writer's emotional involvement in an experience—the why-to of fishing literature. Yet, as Craig Woods observes in his Prologue to this collection of stories, good writing tends to blur the distinctions. An author's philosophical stance or his emotional reaction to some discovery is likely to mark a good how-to article, while a good mood piece is often instructive in some way. None of these types is intrinsically bad or intrinsically good. A well-executed example of any of these forms should be cherished.

A measure that distinguishes bad from good is how much of himself the writer puts into the work. With where-to, the worst manifestations come from the traveling pillagers with their pens, sounding like Chamber of Commerce flacks, producing sickeningly glossy descriptions of angling abundance; the best pieces come from people whose writing shines with deep-felt love for the particular water or area they are describing. With how-to pieces, the worst examples are those tired rehashes of older ideas; in the best how-to writing, the excitement that the author felt in exploring the wonderful complexity of fly-fishing is evident. Maybe mood pieces—the why-to writing—are the hardest to evaluate. The bad examples are too slick, trying too hard to play on a particular emotion; the best ones avoid manipulation, the writer simply offering a bit of himself to the audience (when reading a classic piece of why-to, a person can feel like a witness to a confession).

The three types of writing—why-to, where-to, and how-to—are not equally popular in any era. Readers seem to go through cycles, and publishers of magazines and books try to capitalize on these preferences by pushing out a flood of one type of writing (and in the process they often ride the horse until it dies).

The why-to, mood writing reached a modern peak in the years between World War I and World War II. Masters such as Edmund Ware Smith (*The One-Eyed Poacher of Privilege,* 1936), Philip Wylie (*The Big Ones Get Away,* 1939), and Howard T. Walden II (*Big Stony,* 1940) created works that were widely recognized in the literary world. Any enthusiast of angling literature might well name three other masters—or perhaps twice as many—for the period produced works to suit a variety of tastes. One can choose among many favorites, and one can also speculate on the many conditions favoring such rich periods of sporting literature.

But after World War II such writing suffered a decline. Most of the fault must go to the magazine and book publishers, who recognized the hunger of the reading public for how-to material (and the dollars to be made from satisfying that hunger). They pushed a deluge of very straightforward, nuts-and-bolts how-to stuff at the expense of subtler, better-written pieces. Thus the market for evocative, thoughtful pieces, and for the writers of such pieces, dwindled. There was a period of at least a decade when it was really hard to sell such work.

Fortunately, the trend began to move toward mood writing. There were fine writers who, even when grinding out the basic how-to formula, paid homage to some of the old masters. These allusions created a small but fanatic interest in the classic books—a fact not lost on editors. Also, there were new editors appearing who appreciated the growing sophistication of the post-War, college-educated audience. A few new magazines, especially fly-fishing magazines, came into existence to cater to this expanding market. And there were a few ventures into the publication of sophisticated general-interest sporting periodicals such as *Rod & Gun* and *The American Sportsman*. The latter periodicals were short-lived and perhaps ahead of their time, but they added to the whetting of the public appetite for fishing literature.

What is the future for mood pieces? The first renaissance of why-to writing came when World War II veterans began entering their middle-aged years; now the baby-boom generation, that great bulge in the population charts, is beginning to enter middle age also. Many of these individuals have advanced beyond the stage of wanting to prove their prowess as anglers. It might not be fair to say that they are less passionate in their pursuit of fish, but certainly as a group they are more reflective sportsmen. They have learned to appreciate the game of angling for more than just the fish—and they will also be the kind of readers who can savor a finely crafted, evocative piece of writing.

A successful publisher or editor must be constantly aware of what the public wants to read. In both the magazine and book publishing industries, the better editors have taken note of this renaissance of genuine fishing literature—and of the public appetite for it. Moreover, as I noted earlier, some new editors—young but with a sophisticated taste for the work of fine angling writers—have been employing their talents in support of the new wave. Included among them are the co-editors of this book, Craig Woods and David Seybold, both still in their early thirties but already well seasoned in the publication of evocative sporting literature. I think it is significant that these two editors are, themselves, fly fishermen as well as writers.

David Seybold first cast a fly more than twenty years ago on a small pond on the North Shore of Long Island, New York, where he spent his youth. Since then he has put a fly rod to effective use in a great many places. Now a full-time freelance writer and editor, he lives in the Kearsarge region of New Hampshire, close to what he calls "the perfect lake for trout and landlocked salmon." He has written numerous articles on fly-fishing and hunting, and is currently working on a book of short stories set in New England.

Craig Woods was born in Ohio but can probably be called a true Vermonter, having lived and fished in the Green Mountain State for almost a decade. A former associate editor for *Fly Fisherman* magazine, he is the author of *The Fly Fisherman's Streamside Handbook,* published by Ziff-Davis in 1981. Although he now writes and edits in several outdoor fields, he manages his time well enough to remain an avid angler—and to continue his freelance writing and editing of fishing literature. During the past three years, in fact, he has edited a number of fly-fishing books by various angling authorities.

Two better-equipped editors could hardly be found to compile a book such as *Waters Swift and Still.* The Prologue by Craig Woods and the Epilogue by David Seybold demonstrate that they not only appreciate good writing but also can contribute to it. This collection of new stories is testimony to their fine judgment and to the renaissance of genuine angling literature.

Surely the time is right for this kind of book, and in my opinion, this is the right book for the time. In its pages are some of the best mood writers of our era.

Many of these men are personal acquaintances. Moments shared with them are among my cherished memories: a morning with Nick Lyons in his New York City apartment, a day with Ernest Schwiebert on the Big Hole River, or an afternoon with Charles Waterman in his winter home in Florida. On all of these occasions we talked about the art of writing as much as the art of fly-fishing. The fact that these men truly know the art of writing is well demonstrated in their contributions to this book.

There are older writers I have not met who are still my friends. After all, when you grow up with a person's articles and books he is first your hero and then your teacher. Anyone who is worshipped so devoutly by the boy remains an idol to the man. Individuals such as Lee Wulff and Robert Traver are in this class—and their stories here remind me again how well they write.

Some authors are so good that their names alone make a magazine or book worth buying. Even one piece by men such as Art Lee, John Randolph, Nelson Bryant, Steve Raymond, or John Merwin guarantees that there will be something special—and to have them all in one book is a reader's feast.

Two writers fairly new to me in this collection are Geoffrey Norman and Charles Gaines, but their stories, sensitive portrayals of their development as anglers, leave no doubt about why they belong in any book of this type.

I have my favorite pieces among this collection. There is no need for me to list these stories by preference because this is not a contest. The ones that appeal to me most do so because they touch a secret pain or joy within me. In "Home Waters," by Charles Gaines, there is an opening line that actually hurts, ". . . my father and I rarely got along anywhere but in a fishing boat." That man is my mirror.

In "City Angler," by Nick Lyons, the struggle of an outdoorsman torn between two life-styles is equally evocative. When I was a child in Hartford, my parents let me fish so much because it was the only time I was not getting into trouble. Upon reaching adulthood, it was my decision to make; the time had come to choose city life or country life. In my case, I ran like hell.

"October: A Northwest Idyll," by Steve Raymond, brings sweet reflections simply because the month seems to affect us in the same way. The fishing in these weeks becomes a ritualized order, as if the ritual will somehow slow down the passage of the golden month—but it never does.

If someone else were to select favorites, the list would be different—and that is the way it should be. All the stories in this book are beautifully written. Each of them will pluck at the memories—bitter or sweet—of certain readers. Anyone who has gained the wisdom of a few years on the water will find enjoyment in this many-sided collection.

Prologue
Craig Woods

THERE is a practice among editors and writers of fishing stories to place almost all such stories in one of two broad categories: "how-to" stories and "mood" stories. The former teaches you something, and the latter entertains you. I have come to believe that this classification is as necessary as it can be misleading. It is unlikely that a well-written how-to story about fishing would fail to entertain you, and it is just as unlikely that a well-written mood story would fail to teach you something.

I remember taking a college English course wherein the professor explained that Izaak Walton's *Compleat Angler* provided an excellent sample of Seventeenth Century pastoral prose style. Other than that, he said, there was not much to delve into—unless, of course, you wanted to learn how to fish or how to prepare the fish you had caught. It seems that the close relationship between the how-to and the mood in fishing writing is not a unique characteristic of modern outdoor writing.

But we do need handles for things, and if writers and editors spent all their time discussing semantics, the stories, magazines, and books about fishing that we enjoy so much would not be written or produced.

And so, here goes: This is a book of mood stories, a book designed to entertain you. Yet David Seybold and I would not have brought this book together if we had not felt that you would learn something important about fishing from it. Each of the stories in this book is new, and we have worked with the authors to provide stories that explore different facets of the sport of fly-fishing.

There is variety in this book, and yet we feel that these twelve stories, when taken together, make a cohesive statement about fly-fishing. It's an impressionistic cohesion, to be sure, but that seems all the more appropriate when you consider the manifold nature of the sport.

We also feel that the long tradition of fine writing that is associated with fly-fishing is alive and well, and such writers as those who appear in this book are a part of that tradition.

The contributors to *Waters Swift and Still* find something special in the sport of fly-fishing. In the same sense, perhaps, that they enjoy writing about fly-fishing, we enjoy reading about it. And this hints at why fly-fishing has generated its own literature, why a book such as this is possible. There's a comfortable bond between reader and writer, a sort of knowing wink that indicates a common awareness of the bottom line: Fly-fishing is fun.

David Seybold and I hope you enjoy reading this book as much as we enjoyed our part in bringing it to you.

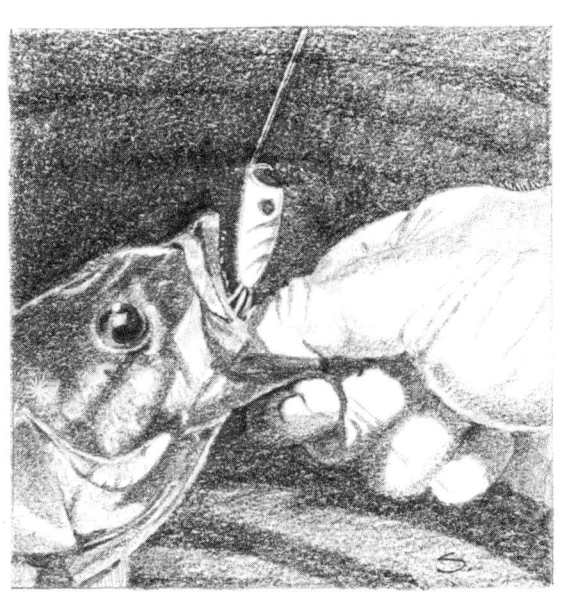

The Way of Consolation

Art Lee

The Way of Consolation

WHEN THINGS go wrong, I can get cranky, and its's best to ignore me until the mood passes. Not that I blame anyone for a foul-up, not down deep. The mood represents some measure of consolation, and to take it from me by saying something chatty makes me feel cheated. Usually I let fly. I don't like crankiness in myself any better today than yesterday or twenty years ago, but time has made it neither easier for me to control nor more pleasant to deal with for those who love me. The fact that some people who loved me twenty years ago still love me, even though they keep saying chatty things at the worst times, is more consolation than I really have coming.

"Look at the mountains, Art. There's fresh snow," Kristin tried. "And a flight of swans. Look, please." Doddi, our Icelandic ghillie, smiled, which is more dangerous than being chatty. He understood almost no English. Such a person is a perfect target.

"The only mountains I want to see are the ones at home." I hated myself for the words even as they were escaping. But I was rolling now. "At least there's no snow. It's August." Kris said nothing. Doddi's smile died. Part of me wished one or the other of them would tell me to knock it off, not that it would have done any good. "I don't believe it," I pressed. "We're supposed to fish salmon. Wait a year . . . travel four thousand miles . . . and what happens? It's screwed up."

"Doddi says the trout fishing's really good," Kristin tried again.

"Trout good. Very many big trout," the Icelandic guide tried, struggling to manufacture an English sentence.

"You don't come to Iceland to fish trout," I spat. "If I wanted trout, I'd fish sixty feet behind my house." Still glaring, I thumbed Doddi's way. "Sure, he'd claim there are big trout. He screwed up the salmon fishing."

"That's not fair, love," Kris said in a tone reserved for times when I'm acting like the original jerk.

Anybody prone to crankiness can testify each outburst costs you. My tab that morning would be to miss being first to sight Laxá I Laxádalur as our van topped a steep incline in the ground-lava road. Kris saw it first, and her expression softened instantly to reflect its beauty. Her face read like opening lines from a favorite book, reassuring you you're safe now from ugliness, even in yourself. "Look," she ordered, pointing past my head, and I turned slowly and sat in silence.

Long silences come naturally when greeting Laxá I Laxádalur for the first time. The only thing you might want to say is that you've found the most beautiful place on earth. But such a sentiment is best held until later. At first, it's better to enjoy a full fantasy of this as your place to live with every day, until one day, somehow fixed yet nonspecific in the fantasy, you die here and are buried deep in a grassy hillside overlooking one of the river's emerald pools.

"I hate you for seeing it first," I said finally.

"You hate yourself for making me see it first," Kristin replied.

Laxá I Laxádalur translates literally to Salmon River in the Salmon River Valley, although this stretch of river and its valley are situated above a falls impassable to the runs of Atlantic salmon that teem into the lower river, called Laxá I Aðaldal, or Salmon River in the Main Valley. Because Laxá I Aðaldal may be the world's finest salmon fishery today, sportsmen, both Icelandic and foreign, have singled it out among Iceland's many *laxá*'s (*laxá* means salmon river, *lax* being salmon and *á* meaning river) to be called simply the Laxá. In the northeast of the island nation, the river rises in Mývatn, meaning Gnat Lake, third largest in

Iceland, and flows almost due north about twenty miles as a duck flies to salt water in the form of Skajálfandifloi, or Wide Fjord that Trembles, just west of Húsavík, a fishing port of some two thousand hearty folk. Within the twenty miles between its source and the North Atlantic, the Laxá actually meanders and tumbles about thirty-five miles through a route of least resistance cut in ancient lava, the stuff Iceland is made of. Of this water, more than half is located upstream of the impassable falls at Laxárvirkjun, the gateway so to speak, to Laxá I Laxádalur.

At the valley entrance there is a steep slope of several hundred feet on each side of the river. Flat on top, the hills are brown and very rocky near their summits, but about a third of the way down, though still well above the level of the road, the barrenness gives way to blueberry bushes and lush grass embroidered with clusters of wildflowers of white and purple and pink. Scattered all about, but particularly near the riverbanks, are natural totems of lava, some tinted gray, bronze, or light green by delicate lichens. There are no trees.

High overhead, puffy clouds rush by, pushed by arctic winds that carry clear, dry air to the north of Iceland during its short summer. The winds have flattened the hilltops until they look almost like tables draped with cloths that ripple where erosion has worn narrow burns in the sides to accommodate snow runoff that even the spongy, volcanic soil won't absorb. High on the slopes, you spot dots of white, brown, and black, which you soon make out to be sheep let out to pasture by farmers who live on the bottomland farther up the valley. Usually the sheep are in pairs, but occasionally there are three together—a ewe and twin lambs, a sign of a farmer's good fortune, according to Doddi. You seldom see the great rams with their curved horns, however, because they wander off into remote areas to live out their summers in bachelor colonies. Many sheep in this valley, although he doesn't say so, belong to Doddi's family, which owns several good farms on the east bank of Laxá I Laxádalur.

Thanks to Doddi, whose real name is Thórdur Pétursson, Kris and I had fished salmon many times along the river's lower reaches, and until the previous evening had thought we were to fish there again—ten days on choice beats. For this trip, though, I'd made arrangements with a farmer friend, believing his English and my Icelandic sufficiently sophisticated to communicate. Doddi, although wondering certainly how I could pull it off when to get just one day's fishing is tricky between fluent Icelanders, friends or not, nevertheless must have guessed everything was set, or was too polite to interfere. We ended up with only a few half days of salmon fishing just before the season closed.

Superior guides possess a common sense of their sport's priorities, and so it didn't surprise me when Doddi, who had again begun his van, a Spanish model built on a Jeep chassis, suggested, "We fish brown trout now. Go *Veidahús* . . ." His English failed him, but he compensated beautifully by sticking his wristwatch in front of my nose and describing three clockwise circles with his index finger.

"Go *veidahús* later?" I responded to the charade.

"*Já*," Doddi nodded, using an Icelandic word for yes. "We fish brown trout. Go *veidahús*, eat *hádegisverdur*."

"Lunch?" I guessed correctly. Doddi repeated the English word deliberately, as if filing it for frequent use. "Eat brown trout for lunch at the fishing house in a few hours," I confirmed. He nodded his head happily and signaled he'd like the sentence repeated. We volleyed it back and forth several times until he indicated his satisfaction with a single, self-assured nod.

Rounding a wide turn in the road, Doddi braked the van, shifted down two gears with practiced efficiency, and rolled into an almost imperceptible pull-off backed by a grassy lane that wound among sculptured outcrops of lava. The river lay hidden beyond the lava that scientists say was deposited about one hundred thousand years ago, but Doddi pointed in its general direction and declared with an authority borne of growing up with a fishery, "Plenty good place. Art Lee catch plenty big brown trout." He flashed a knowing look I'd come to recognize as part bighearted smile, part cat-choking-on-canary, and I realized his singular good humor and confidence were infectious. My petulance had evaporated without me being entirely aware of it, and had been replaced by a sense of anticipation, a mood essential to initiate all thoroughly satisfying angling experiences.

The Way of Consolation

To diagnose why I'd rebel at the prospect of Icelandic trout fishing on one hand, while on the other I'd tote three trout rods, a vest full of trout flies, and a laminated-wood landing net to Iceland is probably best reserved for an analyst. But I should point out that it would never occur to one who carries fly rods to marlin grounds and bass bugs on trout-fishing trips to leave his trout-fishing gear behind when going salmon fishing, if only for its value as a symbol of upward mobility to redcaps who charge by the bag.

About twenty minutes were required to rifle through duffles and rod cases before I stood ready to leave the van and follow Doddi along a snarl of trails beaten into the lava by generations of cloven hooves. Never one to push, the ghillie paused frequently, stooping to pick handfuls of plump blueberries, which he popped into his mouth like a kid eating popcorn. And producing an empty sandwich bag from his windbreaker, he advised Kris with his remarkable gift for pantomime that lunch at our fishing house on this day and for the days to come would be infinitely more appealing if she considered it part of her daily routine to keep the bag full. Kris accepted the bag and the chore with a grin, and we continued meandering until we reached the crest of a knoll where Doddi suddenly halted, folded his arms across his chest, and announced, "Laxá."

For hundreds of days on scores of rivers, I've sought trout and salmon pools the way some travelers seek cathedrals, and somehow each one I'm shown becomes at once the most splendid of all for the wonder of knowing I'm yet to explore it. For, if it's true that the essence of fishing lies concealed in its endless occasions to exercise hope, then the embodiment of this ideal must swim in the waters that glide by under your gaze, awaiting only your presence to begin dramas for which nature has rehearsed the waters for ages.

Laxá I Laxádalur, barely fifty feet below us, shimmered under the climbing sun. Upstream it swung through a narrows in a sharp bend between bluffs and then flattened out into a broad slick etched with tiny currents that betrayed its uneven bottom of bronze bedrock and black lava dust deposited during spring spates. Only the faintest slithering sound was carried on a breeze that seemed to dip and touch the river's surface. From our vantage on the knoll, we could see serpentine growths of weed hanging loosely in the flow. The abundant weed, which reveals the incredible fertility of this river, gives Laxá I Laxádalur the look of an emerald chalkstream or spring creek, unique, as far as I know, among all waters of the arctic region.

What I lacked in grace I surely made up with abandon as I scrambled down the steep path to the riverbank. Odds are better than even that no Icelandic sheep pursued by arctic foxes could have made faster time. Doddi trailed at his casual pace with Kris in tow, both laughing mightily at how the itch to have at the river had clearly supplanted my better judgment, and by the time they caught up, a big Black Ghost streamer, dug from an old, leather fly wallet, was already cinched to my leader tippet. I thought I was ready to go.

"No good," Doddi said soberly after examining the terminal tackle.

"Black Ghost no good?" I asked, throwing Kris a skeptical glance. River by river, everywhere I'd fished big brown trout, this pattern of black, yellow, and white had proven the most reliable, particularly in large sizes.

"*Nei*, Black Ghost plenty good," Doddi asserted, shaking his head impatiently. He grabbed my 2X leader. "No good," he repeated, indicating the tippet. Doddi dug into his fishing vest and produced a spool of fifteen-pound-test monofilament spinning line. "Good," he declared, pitching me that same single, self-assured nod he'd used a half-hour earlier when he meant to convey that further work with my English sentence was neither required nor desired.

"This plenty strong enough for big brown trout," I insisted, flourishing the tippet while raising my right arm to mimic a bodybuilder showing off a bicep. Doddi looked cool, even remote, like an old farmer being told how to plow his fields by a visiting ag-and-tech professor. "I ain't about to hunt quail with a goose gun," I said to reinforce my argument by introducing linguistic one-upmanship, and when Doddi's look became only skeptical, which is the biggest alteration I would have hoped for, I pronounced, "We go. Fish brown trout now," in the most preemptive

The Way of Consolation

tone I could muster. After an instant of mutual indecision, the guide shrugged, and smiling, said something in Icelandic I suspect would relate to losing battles but winning wars. He waited several seconds for sufficient bewilderment to register on my face, and motioned me to follow up along the bank to where Laxá I Laxádalur emerged below the narrows.

We edged into the water and sloshed side by side through the knee-deep flow toward center stream. Perhaps twenty yards in, the rutty bottom began sloping, until about a half-dozen more strides put us in to our waists. Doddi studied the opposite bank, apparently searching out a marker, and when he was satisfied, he grunted and leveled his arm in front of me to draw me up. The ghillie said nothing but gestured with the same arm to angle my fly across and down and to edge downstream a few feet after each cast.

"Long cast? Short cast?" I asked, stripping fat spirals of line from my reel.

"Long cast," Doddi confirmed, snatching the streamer from me and dunking it to soak up the marabou wing. "Okay," he said, releasing the fly.

I twirled it into the air with an abbreviated roll cast, and shooting line fore and aft in a couple of false casts, pitched the big streamer about sixty feet across the current. The flow bellied the line almost immediately, and the upstream mend I made to compensate served not only to right the drift but to twitch the Black Ghost like a darting fish. A swirl materialized almost at once behind the fly, a small swirl, perhaps, by salmon-fishing standards, but a suck-in-your-breath swirl by the standards of a trouter accustomed to the Catskills. I felt nothing. Doddi shot me a smug look. "Small," he clucked.

Responding involuntarily to Doddi's voice, I glanced sideways, and in the instant my attention was drawn off the water, a second swirl had been left behind by a fish that jolted me back to business by picking at the streamer. I measured the trout between the disappearing rings and managed, "Big."

"Very big," Doddi murmured, screwing up his face boyishly as if we'd broken his mother's best vase. He motioned me to pick up the spent cast and to try again, and when the fly had plunked to the surface and disappeared within inches of where it had touched down the first time, he nodded approvingly. After a mend, the streamer turned slowly, its wing breathing with little nods telegraphed through the line from my rod tip. An eternity of tension swam through me while the fly described its arc, and I'm not sure how long it was before I realized Doddi was whistling softly, his way, I guess, to vent the agony of waiting.

The fly reached the tail of its drift unscathed. Except for the pattern of currents and little ripples left by the breezes, the river might have held no living thing. I was preparing to lift my line to start another cast, but Doddi suddenly laid his hand heavily on the rod, as if a voice carried across a thousand years of living with this river had called out from below. *"Beddu augnablik*—Wait awhile." The pressure of Doddi's hand held the rod close to the surface, and I almost complained, but the stiffness of his body and the intensity of his stare at the spot where my fly hung suspended just inches deep, warned me to back off. My eyes passed from Doddi to the line, which I followed downstream to the point where it disappeared. I remember a gust of wind touched down all at once, sending long fingers of broken water across the surface. It was gone as quickly as it had come, leaving us surrounded by stillness.

The pool was becalmed, unnaturally calm for as far as you could see, when the trout's head burst through the surface, pushing six-inch swells to either side. Framed by the swells, the head seemed to me gigantic, dwarfing the wing of marabou that spilled from one side of its open mouth. The inside of the mouth looked white and smooth like china, but the head was bronze and appeared suspended above the surface in the beginning of an even, unworried, effortless roll that would finally carry the head downward, exposing broad, spotted shoulders and flanks, a long, muscular back, and, at last, a tail as big as a man's hand.

The trout's roll propelled it to the bottom. Although gripped in the spell of its roll, as the fish sounded, I raised my rod to my face like a soldier saluting with a sword, a gesture unnecessary to set the hook. The force of the strike had carried more than enough punch to lock the hook

The Way of Consolation

into the trout's rubbery cheek, and like a brawler hit a good one, the fish stopped cold with the sting of it and shook its head violently from side to side.

To play big fish in moving water, it's a mistake to remain in deep where the fish is in its element and you are out of yours. Standing waist deep is to trust Lady Luck, from whom you should presume nothing once she's brought you and your fish together. When a fish has room to run, particularly downstream, to expect to park yourself and drag it back through the current like some dumb cod is an insult to a good river and to a worthy opponent.

"Ashore," I said to Doddi, turning and pointing at the bank. The ghillie nodded, and we began retreating slowly, as we had many times when attached to salmon, Doddi's arm across my back to be sure I kept my balance.

For all the movement of the big trout, I might have snagged the bottom. Line droned off the reel, the result only of our withdrawal. The fish was lying virtually motionless, an anomaly for a hooked trout, large or small. Ten feet off the bank the nail knot that spliced my fly line to the backing ticked through the last couple of snake guides and passed the tip-top, and yet, except for the gentle arc in the rod and an occasional thump reported to my hand when the trout turned its head, there might have been no fish attached.

Aren't you the gallant, I thought, *waiting until the guy you're gonna chew up takes off his tie and hangs up his coat? There you are, shaking your head and saying, "Any old time." Oh, you'd like to look bored enough with it to lose your temper without losing your dignity. Yessir, you're a piece of work. You really think I need this guy's arm around me to stay out of the drink? Not likely. But if it makes you happy to think you're giving me a break, go right to it. If there was a chance, though, just this much chance that I'd end up upside-down tomorrow in Kristján's smokehouse, you think I wouldn't be kicking your* afturhluti *from here to Mývatn?*

But then, you're thinking, "I'm a trout, and he's a man. Worse yet, he's an American. Fat head, like his wallet. Mind turned to mush with too many martinis."

Waters Swift and Still

You didn't know great-grandad Billy, did you? Or about the Irish in me? Heard of the fever sheds? Or the signs: "No Irish Need Apply." Know what Billy used to say? He used to say, "The only thing you can thank luck for is the number of miles you were born from a racetrack." Ran a saloon, Billy did. Never touched a drop himself. Guess what killed him. Fell down an elevator shaft. So whaddaya suppose was chiseled into his tombstone? "Billy Lee," it says, "Who was he anyway?" If you ever get to Riverdale, look it up.

So, be complacent if you want to. But while we've been having this little chat, don't look now but I've been sneaking downstream. The Irish in me. Opposite you, now, right where I oughta be. Gonna make hors d'oeuvres out of you, Krissy and Doddi and me, one week from today, after Kristján's through. Wash you down with good cold mjolk. *Can't afford gin in Iceland. If I could, think you and I would ever come to this? No. You'd be reading the sagas and, me, I'd be fishing salmon downriver someplace, maybe Arnes, at three thousand bucks a week.*

When the trout bolted, its power and speed defied description as a run. Although it involved running, only a fool could read cowardice into it. This fish betrayed no panic, no indecision typical of lesser trout. In terms of human conflict, it seemed as though the fish wasn't in flight at all, but instead that it was coming on, bulling in, determined to give better than it took. Backing seethed off the reel and spat sparkling droplets into the air where it cut the surface. My rod bowed like a palm under a tropical storm. Doddi whooped. I held on.

"Go Laxárvirkjun," Doddi crowed, pointing downriver.

"Gotta chase," I said. The climbing pitch of the reel warned that about half of my backing was already spent. "Can't turn him, Doddi," I moaned. "Won't stop, the sonofa. . . ."

Like two seals running on land, Doddi and I turned and scrambled the rest of the way to shore. At the bank, while still trying to point my rod at the fish, I had to drop to my knees and claw my way up to level ground. But there I staggered upright and began running, my legs and lower torso seeming lost in my cavernous waders. About thirty feet downstream, I have been reminded, I collided with Kris, but I recall neither tossing her aside nor the imaginative expletive she conjured up in keeping with the occasion. All I remember is the hollow sound made by my boots on the grassy turf, as if to furnish rhythm behind the ratcheting reel and the whine of line taut in the wind.

A ridge of lava suddenly materialized in front of me, and the impact of its presence there to block my way struck me an almost physical blow. The ridge ran all the way to the riverbank in a graceful arc that once, perhaps, was the stretch's high-water mark. At the bank it disappeared into a deep hole, its substance eroded by ages of lapping and swirling water. Blocked, I stopped, and the gap between the trout and me continued to widen.

I've never boxed, but I've watched the faces of boxers in the ring, and there's a look—it's in the eyes—that tells you when a fighter knows he's beaten. It may appear just an instant before he's decked, or he may carry it from the first round to the final bell, if the loser goes the distance. The look is washed into the eyes from deep inside the being, maybe from as deep as the soul, and slowly it spills over onto the face and then downward until the entire body is bathed in the inevitable. The look represents, I guess, the ultimate truce between intellect and spirit, and when you recognize it in a fighter, it's hard not to look away, embarrassed for intruding into a man's communion with reality.

At the foot of the lava ridge, I inched to the lip of the hole. Mercifully, there was no room beside me for Doddi or Kristin to stand. They stood in silence behind me, seeing only the back of my head. Almost empty, my reel had reached an impossible pitch, a sound as shrill as a scream of despair, and I was peering down into the hole, trying to wish away the water, when the trout jumped in the tail of the slick. It lugged the fly and the leader, the full weight of the line and the backing, and yet it leaped full-body clear of the water. It jumped still going away, cutting the surface with almost no splash, and on its way back down to the bottom, the big fish broke off.

I was standing in silence, beginning mechanically to crank in my fly line and backing, when Doddi whispered almost tenderly, *"Veidahús?"*

Waters Swift and Still

"Okay," I answered, still cranking, searching the horizon for a smile.

Late that night, I jotted a postcard to my brother: ". . . wonderful trout fishing. Caught a dozen or so, two to six pounds. Fifteen miles of river to ourselves. Lost a monster this A.M. Had it on just long enough to weigh it. Weighed too much for a 2X tippet. . . ."

Gamboling at Frenchman's

Robert Traver

Gamboling at Frenchman's

SHOW ME a fly fisherman who's still out there flailing away—after all, a few faint-hearted ones occasionally do go back to golf—and I'll show you one of the biggest gamblers outside Las Vegas. And one just as heedless of the odds against him. For who but a real gone compulsive gambler would continue to stand for hours, often up to his whizzle-string in ice water, pelting out a series of bent pins adorned with bits of fluff and tinsel, all in the wistful hope that some hungry fish might finally mistake one of them for something good to eat?

My fishing pals and I know quite a bit about all this, for not only do we pursue one of the wariest creatures in all fishdom, the wild brook trout, but we do so in one of the toughest spots we've run across in the whole Lake Superior area of the rugged Upper Peninsula of Michigan, good old Frenchman's Pond, simply Frenchman's to the sturdy crew who regularly haunts the place, of which I am a charter member.

Just to list a few of the odds against fishing Frenchman's is enough to drive the average fisherman back to his golf cart—if not up one or the other of the tall spruces and tamaracks that line the rear margins of its boggy banks. First of all it really isn't a true pond at all—which are quite tough enough to fish anyway, heaven knows—but rather a shallow, crystal-clear and long-abandoned old beaver dam, which, with the aid of

Waters Swift and Still

our annual patching jobs, still backs up its chilly waters for nearly a mile.

The moods of this pixilated pond are as variable as its width and winding course, and both are as eccentric as a midwinter rabbit trail through a cedar swamp. At one point it's but an easy fly cast to reach a riser on the other side; at another, both luck and prayer must accompany the final heave.

Wading is out because of the generations of accumulated silt, which must date clear back to the last glacier. Canoeing we quit when it early swept over us that in all that clear, shallow water any half-decent trout promptly spooked and went into a sulk at the first dip of the paddle. Floating in an inflated tube we put on probation for a spell, despite the accompanying clouds of churned up silt, till the day we flatly banned the tube when a nodding Hal had to be lassoed and towed ashore still bediapered in one, where it took most of a bottle of bourbon to start him cussing again.

"Wee touch of hypothermia from all those cold underwater springs," Doctor Lou diagnosed as he administered still another belt of bourbon to his shivering patient.

"Whatever in hell I've got, Doc, the treatment's too damned expensive," Hal finally croaked. "Imagine flooring nearly a bottle of *that* and not even knowing it."

Short of fly-casting from a balloon, an idea we periodically dallied with, this left us only the pond's boggy banks from which to fish. These ran virtually the length of the pond on both sides, and while there was generally room enough to cast a fly without snagging one of those rearguard spruces or tamaracks, the big feat was to work oneself successfully into position to attempt one.

For both shorelines are composed almost entirely of countless wobbly hummocks rearing their grassy heads out of a hidden multitude of lurking mudholes, still further disguised by blankets of low matted bushes, each tentacled branch endowed with a passion for snapping off artificial flies or weaving eccentric spider-web patterns out of fragile leaders and tippets.

Lloyd summed it up the day we finished building our log cabin on a bare granite knoll overlooking the pond, a cabin complete with an old school bell that would tell even the farthest-wandering fisherman that the late-afternoon cocktail hour had arrived. "Fellas," Lloyd said, pointing pondward during a between-drink lull, "trying to cast a decent fly out there is tougher than playing that old kid's game of rubbing your belly while patting your noggin."

Still we persisted, and the sight of all six of us engaged in our fishing devotionals at the same time moved some of our nonfishing cronies to occasional bursts of poetry.

"Know what you guys look like?" one of them one day suddenly cupped his hand and hollered from the open camp doorway.

"No," one of our struggling band hollered back, "I've often wondered."

"Like a herd of stampeding water buffalo."

"Dead wrong," Hal hollered back. "More like a bunch of drunks on a trampoline."

Why would a crew of canny old fishermen continue to haunt such a crazy place, let alone build a camp there? It would be nice to say we were continually drawn back by its sheer rugged beauty, peeking up like a glittering jewel out of those low wooded serpentine hills with their occasional reddish gleams of ancient granite; by the continued ignoring by the choosy trout not only of our favorite flies but of our years of accumulated lore; yes, by the very dare and difficulty of the place—wups, I almost said challenge, a close call.

All this was indeed part of its charm, no doubt, for one likes to think there's still a touch of Thoreau in every fisherman. But the big lure of Frenchman's was something else—its big wild brook trout, mermaid-plump trout we'd known all along were there, trout almost spectral in their taunting elusiveness, ghostly trout we could so rarely lure or ever land when we did. Yet scarcely a day passed when we failed to behold one of their wave-rippling rises—*kerplonk*—and scarcely a week when one of us wasn't left blinking by being abruptly cleaned out—*ping*—surely two of the most exciting sounds in all fishing.

The presence of these magazine-cover trout in our pond was contrary to all the sacred precepts of fishing we'd picked up at our fathers' knees, of course. For hadn't every savvy fisherman learned from boyhood that few wild brook trout in our northern bailiwick ever grew to be more than twelve inches long? Especially when confined to living in old shallow beaver dams where they were so constantly vulnerable to their many natural enemies? And especially those haunting forsaken old beaver dams fed by dozens of bubbling underwater springs pumping gallons of ice water which, as anybody knew, sharply lowered a trout's metabolism, and therefore his appetite, and therefore the growth of any poor stunted creature forced to dwell there? To all of which certified scrolls of fisherman's wisdom Frenchman's continued to have but one teasing response: *kerplonk!*

As for our prevalence of *pings,* these with true fisherman resourcefulness we managed to blame on everything but ourselves: the difficulty of ever luring a really big trout in all that stereopticon-clear water; the companion difficulty of successfully playing and landing one with all those hidden logs and ancient beaver cuttings and miscellaneous snags and roots and weeds and gobs of tenacious algae lurking in all that silt and along those snaggy-bushed shores, especially when fished from a swaying trampoline; the weirdness and unpredictability of the pond's natural fly hatches and the consequent difficulty of ever consistently matching them. On and on our excuses ran. Finally there was our almost helpless tendency, so common to prideful action-hungry fishermen—especially when the fishing is lousy—to keep tying on still more fragile tippets, so that we generally wound up being chronically underleadered.

This fine-leader syndrome that afflicts so many fishermen is not quite as sporting as it sounds. For the longer an angler fishes, the stronger he's apt to feel that the finer his leader the more follows and hits he's likely to get, probably because so few flies in nature come tethered to nylon tails upwards of umpteen feet long. By and by it sweeps over him that his leader might be one of the weakest weapons in the whole fly-fishing arsenal; that, alas, the sad truth is that as yet there *are* no perfect leaders—that is, both perfectly invisible and unbreakable—(though he nightly prays that Dan Bailey or someone out yonder is working on them) and that any leader he uses is an inevitable compromise between attracting more fish and the increasing risk of losing those he attracts.

Good old Hal put it more tersely. "While there's no damn question that our hawser-leadered buddies stand a far better chance of landing a slob once they're on to it," he one day declaimed, "there's also no question that the fine-leadered boys who prefer action over avoirdupois will get on to far more biggies in the first place." He raised his glass. "Maybe the old poet fellow said a mouthful when he wrote: ' 'Tis better to have lured and lost than never to have lured at all.' "

So the *pings* continued merrily until, following a particularly frustrating day five summers ago, we tolled the camp bell and met in an emergency session and vowed to try to solve some of the problems that afflicted us. One of the more obvious ones, of course, was the constant physical difficulty of fishing the place. So we had another round of drinks and talked away and finally passed the hat and, presto, in a matter of weeks had installed twin rough-plank boardwalks running practically the pond's length on both sides. We also built a narrow footbridge to get across on without having to boat or walk way down around the dam. Finally we fashioned and set out a series of wooden casting docks, Lloyd surrendering his precious collection of old wooden beer crates for us to squat on during the frequent ritual of tying on still more tippets.

All this measurably improved both our balance and tempers as it also increased our *pings,* alas. But our growing frustrations kept pace, for in making our improvements we'd also managed to lose our pet alibi for so regularly falling on our fannies—the now largely vanished difficulty of fishing the place. Some elusive thing was still lacking; we knew not what. Things came to a head just four seasons ago last July, on a memorable Saturday. To save time and rhetoric I'll swipe most of the account from my old fishing notes.

Today we turned Frenchman's into a genuine gambling casino lacking only dice girls and slot machines. Here's how it happened.

When we reached camp around noon the pond had gone crazy. Trout were rising and rolling everywhere: big, little, medium. Hal said it looked like a hail of golfballs with a few bricks and horseshoes thrown in. We quickly rigged up and raced for the boardwalks and our favorite casting stations—mine being at a tangled jumble of ancient submerged logs which, in an inspired burst of creativity, we had labeled the Log Jam, located in the narrows just above our new footbridge. Naturally the Log Jam was a great hideout for big trout since they, like their human pals, generally grab up the best spots. Naturally the Log Jam was also one of the main *pinging* centers of the pond.

All of us fished like mad all afternoon until around five when someone mercifully tolled the camp bell. After the first round of drinks we took a creel census, followed by a stunned silence, for nobody but nobody had caught a decent trout. All of us had had plenty of action, though, either being cleaned out at least once on the strike or busted or pulled off during the play.

"Fine bleeping state of affairs," Hal finally said. "Guess we gotta mend our ways."

"How?" somebody asked.

"Like maybe talkin' things over to see what in hell we can do about it," Hal said. "But first another round."

So we had another round and talked things over and were well into the second fifth when we arrived at an intriguing plan. Beginning the very next day and from then on we agreed to place a standing bet on each fishing trip, every time out. The rules were as simple as falling off a trampoline: The guy with the biggest trout ten inches or over would win a buck each from all the others. That was it. All had to be taken on flies, of course, and the fly produced.

During our huddle we kept reassuring ourselves that we weren't even faintly commercializing our favorite sport. Perish the thought. Merely trying to chase away boredom and stimulate zeal in what we all agreed was one of the toughest spots we'd ever fished. Then we had another round and huddled some more and, to add spice to the roll of the dice, further agreed that the losers would pay two bucks a head when the winning trout reached twelve inches or better; three bucks at thirteen and so on into the higher realms of fantasy. We'd simply gamble our way into a state of mingled bliss and more fish.

There were a few miscellaneous odds and ends: A guy could keep his qualifying trout in a live trap, if he liked, and return it after the showdown. Or sooner if meanwhile a pal happened to catch a still larger trout.

"But suppose I catch a twelve-incher and Hal noses me out with a thirteen?" I inquired. "Don't I deserve a two-dollar credit for coming so close or must I also pay Hal three bucks along with the poor guys who only caught a chill?"

"Close don't count, lads," Hal argued in rebuttal. "Main reason I gave up dancing."

So my suggestion was voted down with only my lone dissent. Next we agreed a guy couldn't hog a hot spot all day but was limited to a half-hour at a stretch if another guy showed up and wanted to give it a try. Finally we agreed that each day's betting would end with the ringing of the camp bell, summoning all parched fishermen to the first round of drinks, generally around five.

"To Frenchman's!" Hal toasted at the end of our historic huddle.

"Transformed from pastoral boardwalk to roaring gambling hell all in one afternoon," someone said.

'Twas the last day of fishing and all up and down the pond my pals and I scurried against the deadline at five. Four summers had fled since we'd started gambling at Frenchman's and as I took up my stand at the Log Jam and sat tying up a new tippet my thoughts wandered over the intervening years.

Our fishing had picked up remarkably from the very first day, whether from avarice or added concentration I cannot quite say. One thing was plain: All of us fished longer and harder and with far more intensity. That very first Sunday I'd started at this same spot, hadn't I? Ah, yes, it was all coming back. We'd begun fishing around noon and on just about my first cast at the Log Jam I'd hooked and landed a plump twelve-incher—my first decent trout in weeks—and had admired and calibrated him and reverently placed him in my brand-new live trap.

I recalled how, in my excitement, I'd spent most of the rest of that first afternoon boardwalking up and down the pond proudly telling my pals about my prize—and also making sure that none had excelled me. Then, only minutes before five, Hal had come ambling along and paused to admire my fish.

"Any more luck?" Hal softly inquired.

"Couple small passes," I lied softly, as I'd actually just busted off on an even bigger trout.

"Mind if I give it a try?"

"My pleasure," I further lied, resignedly reeling in and moving away. "Don't catch 'em all."

Before I'd retreated ten paces along the boardwalk Hal had made a few false casts and popped out a little dry over my hot spot and—presto—hooked and splashily fought and landed what turned out to be that first day's winning thirteen-incher. Meanwhile, I, always slow at math, stood there stupidly figuring out that instead of just winning ten bucks (five guys at two bucks a head) I'd just lost three, all in one lousy cast, a total net loss—let's see—of thirteen whole bucks, almost the price of two bottles of our favorite hypothermia therapy.

During those years I'd occasionally won a few bets, of course, for it's hard for anyone to lose all the time at anything, even when the cards do seem stacked against you. And after all, wasn't it just as egotistical to believe in consistent bad luck as in good, both carrying their self-absorbed assumption that someone out there gives a damn? Yes, but wasn't it still mighty curious that most of my few winnings had either been on under-twelve-inch days or only when a few guys showed up?

Gamboling at Frenchman's

And wasn't it only last summer that I'd caught that dreamy plus-fourteen-incher when *none* of my pals had shown up?

I finished tying on my new tippet, then a small dry, at the same time ruefully wondering whether that distant first day of betting hadn't set the tone and pace of my piscatorial gambling career. True, our fishing had sharply improved, mine included, but why in hell did I so rarely win a bet and so often merely come close? Was it some sort of punishment for ever daring to suggest allowing that betting credit? Had my fate as our gang's favorite pigeon frozen me into a permanent role as runner-up?

Kerplonk, I suddenly heard, scrambling up so rapidly I kicked over one of Lloyd's beer crates, stripping and whipping out line, finally lofting out the little dry, which sang past my ear, poised for a fleeting moment, and then settled like a wisp of thistle in the middle of the lovely ebbing circle left by the rising trout.

The trout instantly rose and took the fly. I struck—lo, there was no *ping*—and I all but skidded it out of the danger zone—the narrow Log Jam where all of us so regularly lost so many fish and flies—and in moments had landed it and stood hefting it in my hand—a nice drippy twelve-incher. I glanced at my live trap, and then almost furtively up and down the pond—no pals in sight—and suddenly knelt and slid it back into the water, where it lay working its gills for a moment and then, presto, was gone.

"Maybe that will break the spell," I murmured out loud, feeling for a moment like one of those legendary millionaires lighting up his cigar with a ten-dollar bill.

In the next hour at the same spot I took and returned two more trout about the same size, one possibly larger. Then I sauntered back to camp and sipped a slow can of beer, listened to a couple of innings of baseball, then sauntered down below the bridge to check on my pals. Also to see what in hell was keeping them glued below. Also to show them I hadn't used up my current half-hour at my favorite spot.

Fishing had been good below, too, I discovered, Lloyd having just been cleaned out at the Big Spring and Lou a little earlier at his favorite Weed Patch. Ted and Gigs were still out of sight, probably in the deeper water down at the dam, a sporty big-fish spot the two often shared, while, as usual, good old Hal stood teetering and casting away on a rickety wooden platform on stilts that we called the Diving Board, so I moved down his way.

"Any luck, pard?" I inquired. Hal grunted and gestured at his nearby live trap. "May I sneak a look?" I said, and Hal nodded and I sneaked a look. "Hm," I said, for my hunch had been right: There lay a gorgeous trout, at least a fourteen-incher.

"Want to give my spot a whirl?" Hal said as I turned to leave.

"No thanks, pal, just came down slumming to see what I had to beat."

"Better get going," Hal said, glancing at his watch. "And don't catch them all."

"Have a nice day," I said as I got going, "as total strangers keep chanting at check-out counters as they heist our dough."

Once back at my Log Jam I saw it was already past midafternoon and that time indeed grew short. Play it cool, I told myself. So I sat on my beer crate and went through some of the more chaotic of my fly boxes. Then I heard a good trout rise and glanced upstream and saw its circle spreading over the Top Log area.

Remembering our half-hour rule, I glanced at my watch and headed for the Top Log, pausing a good cast length below the sunken log, which today I could plainly make out running straight out and downward from the brushy shore where, in the distant days when it was still a tree, it had once proudly stood.

First glancing back to make sure my favorite spot wasn't being invaded, I worked out line, false-casting, and finally sailed out a sizable dry just beyond the deeper end of the sunken log over one of the bigger springs. I glanced around to check on my pals and inadvertently twitched the fly and heard a watery explosion and then a sharp *ping*—and ruefully saw I had not only lost my fly but nearly half my lovely tapered leader.

Again I glanced at my watch—my, my, how the time flew—and stood there debating whether I still had time to tie on a brand-new leader or at least a couple of lengths of new tippet. Better get back there first, I told myself, and then we'll see.

Gamboling at Frenchman's

    Back at the Log Jam I'd barely sat down on my beer crate when I almost fell over backwards as a simply whopping trout rose, sending out wavelets in all directions. Once again I glanced at my watch and emitted a whistle—make that a low whistle—and mentally shrugged and found and managed to tie onto the remaining half of my shortened hawser leader a duplicate of the big feather-duster fly I'd just lost.

    "Only minutes more," I kept whispering as I whipped the fly back and forth, back and forth, my fly darting like a hummingbird, all but closing my eyes as I finally released both fly and whirling hawser in the general direction of the Log Jam, where it landed at the far end with a watery *plop*.

    Nothing happened and then I remembered the magic twitch, so I gave my fly a little twitch and a trout rose. I struck, and to my dismay saw I was on to a plucky junior-leaguer that seemed scarcely larger than my fly. Again a glance at the watch—only two minutes more—someone campbound waved at me from the footbridge—so I reeled in furiously, hoping to get in at least one more cast before the final bell.

    I'd skidded the small trout almost to shore when I saw and heard a sudden surging *kerplonk*, and I reared back and struck more out of shock than anything, and found myself latched on to an epic rod-bender that thrashed and churned like a retrieving spaniel.

    The camp bell was still ringing as I finally towed him in close and batted him ashore with my net, for no way would he fit, falling on him and wrestling him just as he disgorged the smaller trout with my fly still in its jaw. Still wrestling, I managed to unhook my fly and slip the still-wriggling junior back into the pond.

    "Looks like a dandy," Hal hollered across from the camp doorway, shading his eyes.

    "Not bad," I modestly hollered back. "May need a licensed surveyor to measure 'im."

    I left my big trout crammed and sulking in the trap, eyeing me balefully, and headed back to camp, now wrestling not with any trout but a flood of vexing questions. Had I really caught this monster on a fly? I asked myself. Or merely on a midget trout I'd already taken on a fly? But we had no rule against trolling or baiting our fly, had we, and wasn't this really akin to maybe adding a lone kernel of corn or a wee salmon egg to one's adroitly maneuvered fly? Or wasn't all *that* a lot of bull and shouldn't I confess all and leave the verdict up to my pals?

"Looks like it's between us," Hal said after we and the other boys had downed our first round. "How big is your baby?"

"Don't know yet, Hal," I answered honestly enough, "but I'd guess at least somewhere between eighteen and twenty inches, maybe more."

"Wow! Whadya catch'im on, man?"

I glanced down at the pond for a spell and turned and answered Hal. What do *you* think I said?

Some Reflections on Failure

Ernest Schwiebert

Some Reflections on Failure

THERE is a story in northern Norway, where the reindeer-moss barrens of the Finnmarksvidda conceal thousands of glacier-scour lakes in the granite highlands, about an abortive fishing expedition made by the Duke of Westminster late in the Nineteenth Century.

His expedition had the comic overtones of Gilbert and Sullivan. Westminster and his family had discovered the fishing at Alta, mooring their steam yacht in the fjord off Bossekopp. Its salmon fishery was once the finest in the world, and Westminster had on one occasion taken more than thirty salmon averaging almost thirty pounds each in a single night's fishing on its Jorahølmen beats.

The British maritime charts of the region suggested that the Reisa watershed, lying between the Alta and the fishing port at Tromsø, was almost as large as the Alta itself. Westminster was excited over the prospect of discovering another Alta in arctic Norway, and he started planning another expedition into its coastal fjords during the winter of 1887. Preparations were extensive, since it was necessary to transport his own supplies and longboats and ghillies. Excitement grew on the voyage from England, bubbling at a fever pitch when Westminster's yacht was finally anchored in the clear shallows of the Reisafjord.

His Norwegian emissary went ashore to bargain with the farmers in the villages, traveling upstream in a Karasjok longboat with some river Lapps while the party waited on the yacht. Westminster and his friends fussed with their tackle. Their ghillies prepared the boats and fittings, sharpened their gaffs and fishing knives and axes, and checked their tents and cooking gear and bedrolls. The anticipation mounted on the yacht.

Finally the emissary returned to the main party. The farmers had agreed to their fishing at a surprisingly low price, and Westminster and his friends congratulated themselves on their venturesome spirit and acumen.

Westminster set out first with his favorite boatman and ghillie, traveling upstream for several days to the Fossholen Pool, where a large waterfall finally stops the run of salmon. His friends followed him at precise one-day intervals. Each boat was poled and rowed patiently to the waterfall campsite, and each angler fished back to the yacht, stopping overnight at the campsites established by Westminster on his pioneer trip downstream. The party was almost military in its precision, with discipline and planning that would have brought pride to the Khyber Rifles.

History tells us they caught nothing and soon abandoned the river to reach their fishing on the Alta. Although Westminster had negotiated a ten-year lease with the farmers at Reisa, which he continued to honor in succeeding years, history also tells us they never went back.

Fifteen years ago I made a similar pilgrimage to Reisa with several Norwegian friends. Our trip was less difficult than Westminster's voyage, since we flew to Tromsø and chartered an Otter floatplane across the beautiful Lyngen Alps into the Reisafjord. My friends had arranged for a stop at one of the big lakes in the Finnmarksvidda to fish for trout and char, and the Otter returned in the evening to complete our flight into the Reisa valley.

The Otter appeared on schedule, roaring on its downwind pass over the rocky island where we were fishing, and circling back in a tight turn to land in the choppy waters of the open lake. The pilot taxied carefully toward the rocky beach, where ancient glaciers had scoured a perfect seaplane ramp, and we loaded our equipment aboard. The trip across the beautiful Lyngen escarpment in the twilight was remarkable, the serrated ramparts almost black against snowfields that glowed in the waning light. We landed on the Reisafjord, cutting its mirror-still surface with our floats, and when we turned the Otter back toward the village a boatman was already stroking rhythmically out to meet us.

We fished the river for three days in seemingly perfect salmon-fishing weather without moving a salmon. *History is repeating itself,* I thought wryly.

Our last morning was still and clear, and we decided to explore the upper beats with the river Lapps. Their Karasjok longboat resembled a racing scull with its bow gracefully curved like a Viking longship, and a stern that had been modified to mount an outboard motor. The last five miles of river to the waterfall flow smoothly over a pale bottom that conceals nothing, and I stood in the boat hoping to spot fish. Our passage revealed nothing in those final miles, and after a discouraged lunch at the Fossholen, during which we saw no fish under the falls, we traveled unhappily back to the fjord.

The Otter was waiting in the twilight to fly us back along the coast to Alta. The fishermen rowed us out to the plane, where the pilot crouched waiting on the floats. We transferred our gear to the cargo floor behind the seats, clambered into the plane, and buckled our seatbelts. It had been a wasted four days on the Reisa, and I was looking forward to fishing the Sautsø beats at Alta.

The engine whined and caught and settled into a deep-throated roar. The pilot steered the Otter expertly with its rudder bar until we faced the open fjord, and sat patiently watching the gauges.

"Why don't you drive?" The pilot asked as he unlocked the control yoke and swiveled the wheel across to my seat. "It's a nice evening and the water's fine."

The pilot locked the water rudders, and after checking the gauges, he raised his thumbs. The Otter shuddered and settled on its floats, and then its huge engine cowling came up and we started our takeoff run. The floats were finally skimming as we gathered speed, lifting in the evening stillness until we were scarcely touching the smooth water.

Waters Swift and Still

The fjord looked like a polished piano lid, and it was growing quite cold, so our takeoff run was relatively short. The floats were barely touching when I rotated, teasing back on the yoke, when an immense disturbance erupted on the surface just ahead of the plane.

"What in hell was that?" I yelled, looking back from our climbing turn. "Did you see that?"

The pilot took the controls and circled back along the darkening fjord. Several enormous wakes disturbed the quiet surface. We pulled back into a tight circle above the wakes and stared like schoolboys. Five whales swam lazily along the fjord, bulging its surface and gliding like ghosts over its pale bottom. Their wakes sliced the water in undulating patterns that caught the soft twilight sky when they finally turned back toward the dark water beneath the cliffs. We turned in the gathering darkness and found the whales were gone.

"Whales!" the pilot said, shaking his head in wonder. "Whales are always exciting!"

"Worth the trip," I agreed.

Such encounters can erase the taste of failure, and a fly-fishing life is filled with similar examples.

My boyhood years offer many bittersweet memories of failure while fishing, from the Catskills to the California coast above San Francisco. These memories are important for the echoes they evoke. Some memories are early, and the first is of a small bass lake in northern Indiana. I was probably about five years old. My father had given me a cheap casting rod and reel, and sometimes he permitted me to play beside the boat with an old Bass-O-Reno. Its chipped red-and-white paint was combined with treble hooks and bulging yellow eyes on a wooden, torpedo-shape plug. It dived when I pulled with the rod, and it bobbed back up to the surface when I stopped. It was fun to play with the bass plug while my father rowed and fished patiently.

The evening I remember passed slowly. My father's casting probed the docks and sailboat moorings along the north shore of the lake. We had fished an hour without catching anything, and I was teasing the Bass-O-Reno just behind the boat when the big bass struck.

There was a great splash that showered the stern. The floating red-and-white plug was engulfed and the cheap reel protested with a shrill rattle. It disgorged a tangle of frayed linen, and the steel rod bucked and plunged in a stalemate. The bass jumped once just beyond the gunwale, looking huge as it showered spatterdock and elodea, and then it sounded behind the boat. The straining rod and tangled line left me helpless and frightened, and suddenly the fish was gone.

There was another boyhood experience on the Smoky Hill in central Kansas, when my parents stopped to visit college friends in those early years. Our host knew that we liked fishing, and he had arranged a nocturnal trip to his favorite stretch of the river.

"Channel catfish," he explained proudly.

The night was quite dark, and the hills beyond the river were merely a dark silhouette against the sky. The river had a surprising current in its labyrinth of channels, and our friend led us along its sandy bars. There were huge tangles of driftwood in the darkness, and my father and I sat around a small fire while the others rigged their trotlines. It grew quite cold just before daylight, and although we failed to catch anything, I will never forget the early light on those flint hills along the river, or the solitary coyote that yelped its brief salute to the coming day.

There were trips for big pike and bass that ended in failure, too. Rain often interfered with our brief vacation trips, and I can remember a camping expedition to Devil's Lake in Wisconsin when it poured constantly. Our tents leaked everywhere. They beaded with moisture and dripped into saucepans and coffee pots until our bedrolls were too cold and clammy for sleeping. Cookfires were impossible, too, and our cuisine was reduced to peanut butter spread on soggy bread, cold canned soup and meat, and powdered milk mixed with rainwater.

When the rain merely fell steadily, instead of coming in sheets that erased from view the forested crater that concealed the lake, we fruitlessly tried trolling and casting for pike and bass. During the sleepless nights, with the heavy rains drumming on the dripping tent, my father's friends tried to bolster our spirits with a comic lullabye:

Rock-a-bye baby, in the tree tops,
While down on the ground—old daddy's a-sops!

Muskellunge obsessed my father briefly, too, and there were several trips to Grindstone Lake in Wisconsin and Mille Lacs still farther north. The spoons and plugs we were sold in the tackle shops at Hayward and Brainerd seemed bigger than the fish we caught. There was a brief encounter with a muskellunge at Grindstone, when an immense shadow stalked a big spoon hung with a shirt-sized pork rind, but the ghostlike fish simply vanished without taking.

"Maybe we should troll the whole pig," the guide suggested. "Them muskies are mean!"

Failure also led directly to my early fascination with fly hatches. I remember many hatches so heavy that I would give almost anything to fish them again knowing what I have learned since. Fishing is still a useful metaphor for life.

There was the blizzardlike sedge swarm on the Little South Pere Marquette in Michigan, when the twilight was filled with egg-laying caddis. The trout had worked steadily before the swarm emerged from the foliage along the banks, but there were no rises during the peak fly activity. Then the trout finally gorged themselves softly at nightfall. Conventional dry flies failed completely on those fish, and it puzzled me for many years. Much later I feel certain that the trout were feeding on hatching caddis pupae in the early evening. There were no rises during the dense mating swarm because the caddis were flying and there were no insects on the water. The soft feeding just at dark was probably to spent caddis, and I wish I could fish that evening again with a spent partridge-wing pattern.

The Firehole offered lessons, too. Its morning rises in late summer were baffling, and there were equally puzzling rises of steadily sipping trout at twilight. During both times of day, there seemed to be nothing on the current, yet the fish were working in a frustratingly steady rhythm. My only success came during the afternoon hatches of tiny *Baetis* flies, but the morning and evening rises remained a puzzle. Subsequent experience on the Firehole and its sister rivers has taught me about the heavy spinner falls typical of their late-summer fishing. The morning rises were probably to tiny *Tricorythodes* spinners, and the twilight feeding had perhaps been focused on mixed swarms of spent *Baetis* and *Pseudocloeon* flies. It would be exciting to test such hindsight.

Still earlier, at the threshold of the Second World War, my father, my uncle, and I spent a frustrating week at Hot Sulphur Springs on the Colorado. The first morning we fished below the village in Byer's Canyon, where the river forces through a fissure in the lava outcrops of the Middle Park. My father and his brother insisted upon starting early, and several bait fishermen were already working their worms and salmon eggs in the deep canyon pools. The bait fishermen had caught nothing, and my father was also unsuccessful with the wet flies he had purchased at Cook's in Denver.

Just before noon, when the sun finally warmed the chill morning in the canyon, the fish started working on the surface. Their feeding quickly settled into a monotonous rhythm. The current was covered with rises for forty-five minutes, and then the rises stopped. No one had caught anything.

"Sure don't want worms," one fisherman said.

"Salmon eggs either," his partner answered unhappily. "And they don't want flies from the look of things."

"The fish are only playing," another fisherman said.

Although I was still quite young I was sure that the fish had been taking *something*, even if we could not see what it was. For many years, I heard other fishermen explain failure with the excuse that the trout were playing. But I resolved that I would try to understand the trout's behavior on such days, and even my limited experience soon left me convinced that the fish lived in a delicate equilibrium between life and death. Their lives offered no chance to play, and our failure at Byer's Canyon led me to a lifetime of exploring fly hatches.

    The plaintive calling of whippoorwills saved fishless evenings during my early summers in Michigan and Wisconsin, and the evening calling of cuckoos once healed my disappointment along the Test at Hurstbourne Priors. There were arctic terns that scolded me for my poor fishing at Skardshylur on the Grimsá in Iceland, and immense flocks of myna birds and monkeys were shrill visitors to our campsite above the Karnali in Nepal. When I failed to solve a rise of fish at Seven Castles on the Frying Pan, it was difficult to sleep because of the bright moonlight and a yelping choir of coyotes in the Colorado hills. The moose that routed me from Blacktail Spring Creek offered some comic relief after I had lost a smutting cutthroat of five or six pounds in those Wyoming bottoms. The Firehole is a river that has beaten generations of anglers, yet its generosity is legend, too, with herds of calving elk in early summer and buffalo in the meadows in the fall, shaggy beasts breathing like hot springs in the chill wind.

    The Henrys Fork is another river with its full measure of failure, even for the regulars who fish it throughout the summer. Its selective rainbows have humbled every fisherman and guide on the river. Days of failure in its lush meadows have been leavened by the clamor of mating sandhill cranes and the river's colony of trumpeter swans. One evening stands out in my memory, when I was fishing the island channels on the

Some Reflections on Failure

Harriman Ranch. Its fish proved particularly moody that day, and when it finally grew dark, our party had been frustrated by a swarm of tiny green-bodied spinners. The others started back along the west bank while I waded across the quiet currents. The dying light was warm on the Tetons far beyond the river meadows on the horizon. There was no wind, and only the soft current sounds broke the stillness.

Suddenly there was the wild sound of geese in the gathering darkness. *Where are they?* I searched the twilight sky for the clamoring flocks. *Where are they?*

The birds came low against the eastern sky, skein after skein weaving and breaking pattern and coming together again. Their cries filled the twilight. The geese did not see me standing in the river as they flared and set their wings and settled. Hundreds of birds splashed down into the current all around me, and still other flocks spilled in until the river and its banks were alive with geese.

It can't have been much different when John Colter first explored these bottoms, I thought. *It's an echo of something we've probably lost.*

I waded silently across the river, slipping behind the screening islands. The geese had settled for the night and scarcely noticed my retreat. I stood silently in the darkness listening to their contented gabble and cacophony before I finally started back.

But my best lesson in failure came recently in a week of salmon fishing on the Grand Cascapedia. I had been invited to join Nathaniel Pryor Reed along with Gardner Grant, Dan Callaghan, and Jack Hemingway.

Just days before it was time to leave for Québec, Reed called with a supplemental invitation. His twelve-year-old son, Pryor, was coming along to fish with us, too, and he asked my twelve year old to join the party. Erik had never fished for salmon, and while we packed our baggage, the house was filled with excitement.

We fished for a week on the Englehard water, staying in the beautiful camp at New Dereen, where the storied Gray Griswold had made his headquarters a half-century before. Our fishing was in freight canoes, with guides taking care of the boat handling and canoe drops on the river, and our weather, if anything, was too good.

The first morning Erik and I drew the Phipps Pools, and just after we had anchored our canoe I rigged a Silver Rat in the mist that shrouded the smooth-flowing river. We had agreed that I would fish the salmon lies that required long casts and that Erik would fish the short-cast drops. While I checked my knots and backing carefully, a huge salmon leaped full length from the pool, and the sound of its immense splash echoed through the fog.

"Daddy," Erik almost whispered with a sense of awe, "was that a salmon?"

"What did you think it was?" I chuckled.

"I don't think I want to catch one," my son said softly, "they're too big!"

"We'll see," I said.

Although it was relatively late in the run, the Phipps Pool had been fishing well and I hooked a salmon on the sixth cast. It exploded in a twisting jump that shattered the stillness, and Erik shouted. The salmon leaped again, its silvery pirouette in a wild halo of spray, and then it ran downstream. The reel became a shrill ratchety solo, and the fish leap-frogged past the granite ledges far below. The guides had pulled the anchor and were following now, our freight canoe running the swift chutes below the pool.

Damn, I thought, as the fish carried us into the rapids, *we're running through Erik's fish*. My fish had bored through his lies in its wild flight downstream, and we did not land the sixteen-pound henfish until we reached the Swallow's Tail, almost a half-mile below where it was hooked.

Although the fish were relatively moody all week, Hemingway and Callaghan quickly adapted their steelheading skills to Atlantic salmon, and Reed killed a cockfish of thirty-odd pounds just above the Rainville

Some Reflections on Failure

Camp. Young Pryor Reed took a good salmon on our third evening, and everyone had finally caught fish during the week except my son. Erik *had* caught a case of depression, a familiar malady among even the most experienced salmon fishermen. His early optimism had ebbed in those first fishless days, and his despair deepened with each new failure.

His luck was consistently bad, and it resulted in the cardinal mistakes of salmon fishing. Erik took the fly away from several salmon. Twice he missed fish when their swirls left him open-mouthed and speechless. His spirits always seemed to brighten when we drew a productive pool, but when he lifted into another cast and took the fly away from a following salmon at the Guest Pool, I saw tears in his eyes and said nothing. Other things went wrong, too, and when a fish missed his fly in shallows where no salmon should have been lying, the guides shook their heads in sympathy. His usual good spirits were less evident at mealtimes, and Erik became dour and unusually quiet.

Late in the week I found him fishing for trout in the boat shallows at New Dereen, perhaps to restore his confidence on a species that he understood better. Several times I saw him staring gloomily at the Cascapedia.

Our week was almost finished. We had carefully fished through the Guest Pool again without luck, and as we were traveling the river toward the lights of New Dereen, I turned to Erik.

"You seem a little discouraged," I said. "What's wrong?"

"Daddy," he said tearfully, "salmon are hard!"

The last morning our host called me into his sitting room after breakfast. Reed was also concerned that Erik had still not taken a salmon, and he outlined a fresh strategy. We had access to another beat upstream that evening. It had not been fished all week, although our guides had made a reconnaissance and reported it filled with bright fish.

"We'll rest it today and hold it for Erik until this evening," Reed said. "He'll get his salmon."

We agreed that Erik was probably feeling too much pressure with my fishing from the same boat, so the last evening he left with young Reed and his father for the promising beat upstream.

I went farther upstream to some dry-fly pools with Hemingway and Callaghan, and just at twilight I hooked a huge salmon that drifted up like a ghost from the ledges and took my fly. It jumped twice, and I was startled at its size and clumsiness. Then it bolted across the river and jumped again. Callaghan came running along the opposite shore, shouting advice while the fish sullenly stripped line.

"You'd best follow him," the guide recommended.

Although the salmon had briefly seemed under control, holding quietly across the smooth flow against a bellying line, it was taking line steadily now. "That fish seems bored," I laughed softly. "But I'd better follow him."

The fish was gathering speed, and I was losing great lengths of line while we scrambled across the ledges to follow. It had stripped the reel deep into the backing. The backing was still dwindling on the spool when I started running along the muddy shallows. The fish threatened to reach the rapids downstream. It was controlling the fight now, and it had consumed most of my backing. It was impossible to follow its flight down the half-mile chutes, and I had tightened to prevent its run when the fly pulled out suddenly.

"Damn!" I said. "He's gone."

"How big was that fish?" Callaghan shouted from across the river. "Did you get a good look at him?"

"Too good," I groaned. "Maybe thirty pounds."

"It's too bad," the guide said.

We drove back along the river to New Dereen, arriving before the rest of our party. We had a whisky on the tackle porch, wondering how the other beats had fished and whether Erik had taken a salmon at Tracadie.

We stripped off our fishing vests and waders, and placed our salmon rods on their pegs under the eaves of the porch. It was getting cold and I was still chilled from wading as I ran a bath in the giant tub. The steaming water felt good, and I settled deep into the suds, savoring the relaxation that filled my senses. My failure with the big Cascapedia salmon was almost forgotten when I heard a wild chorus of horns. It sounded like a wedding coming through the meadow.

Some Reflections on Failure

"They've gone crazy!" Hemingway shouted from his quarters. "I'll bet Erik's got his fish!"

The horns stopped honking and the night was filled with the sounds of laughter and banging screen doors. The bathroom door burst open, and a raucous parade of salmon fishermen came in noisily to slide a twelve-pound henfish into my tub. The boys danced a crazy jig with my towels, and in their shining faces I saw something I never understood as well before: the importance of failure to the sweetness of success.

Catch and Release
and Other Things

Nelson Bryant

Catch and Release and Other Things

THERE is a growing band of American fishermen who regard the keeping of one's catch as something reprehensible. This reaches a peak among fly-fishing trout anglers, and that is easy to understand.

Fish in oceans and large lakes can eventually be decimated by both sporting and commercial interests, but big waters can stand a lot more pressure than a trout stream. In the East, in particular, there are streams, or portions of them, set aside for fishing for fun—all trout to be returned to the water alive—or as trophy streams from which only one or two large fish may be kept.

The intent of this is laudable and the results equally so. There is no way the public sections of certain classic streams in the Catskills, for example, could maintain significant, ongoing trout populations if everyone who fished them was free to bring home a usual limit each day. If special limits or no-kill restrictions were not imposed on such waters, the native fish would soon be wiped out, to be replaced, if funds were available, by pale replicas from a hatchery.

Throughout most of the world, the days of unlimited catches of trout are gone, days such as those at the mouth of the St. John River in Québec described by that well-connected American angler Genio Scott in his *Fishing In American Waters* (1869).

"Our little party," wrote Scott, "continued to take trout [sea-run brookies] at the mouth of the St. John for nearly a week, until a schooner was prepared to take us to the Gaspé. The silver trout is indeed beautiful, being plump and round, with its polished sides gleaming brightly with a satin sheen which sparkles with glowing lustre in the light . . . the only drawback that I experienced in taking silver trout arose from too many of them offering for my flies at a time . . . men, women and children [coastal fisher-folk] followed us along the river and gladly received all the smaller trout . . . it was an easy matter to take in two hours a barrel of trout running from half a pound to four pounds."

Between the obvious excesses (by today's standards) of Scott's experience and the fanatical devotee of no-kill trout fishing lies a compromise. The compromise need not only reside in law, but in the heart of the angler as well.

There was a time, I must admit, when it was important to me to bring home a limit of trout. That urge died thirty years ago. Now, one or two good fish is usually all I want. I only want to bring the wheel full circle, to savor the sweet flesh, perhaps with a friend, of the fish I hold in such high esteem. That, I submit, does not mark me as devoid of sensitivity.

In their understandable urge to protect the fish and good fishing, there are many anglers who have worked around to a position where carrying a creel is the mark of a boor. This is most prevalent, as noted, among fly-fishing trout fishermen, but manifestations of something like it can be found in saltwater angling also.

I know a Boston physician who loves to cast for striped bass in the surf. He catches a lot of fish but returns them all to the water. I have no complaint about him—stripers appear to be in trouble, and the doctor makes no attempt to impose his custom on others. It is entirely possible, also, that he doesn't enjoy eating fish or doesn't want to bother cleaning and cooking them.

My position is that killing a fish is not a reprehensible act, unless, of course, it is a threatened or endangered species. On the other hand, I cannot tolerate those I have observed bringing three dozen ten-pound bluefish to the dock, then tossing them overboard or into garbage cans when the picture-taking is done.

Inflation has affected certain patterns of angler behavior. Some years ago, there were several striped-bass anglers—both surf casters and boatmen—I knew who, when they got into a school of good fish, kept only one or two for themselves or their friends. Today these men keep every fish they catch and sell them. I am sorry this has happened, but I understand the motivation. In this era of an inflated economy, if a man takes time off from work to go fishing and perhaps spends twenty-five dollars for gas running along the beach in his boat, it is unrealistic to expect him not to sell his catch. There were many times in recent years when striped bass were bringing more than a dollar a pound in the round (ungutted) to the angler.

Nor do I quarrel with the fellows who set aside a day to go offshore in a party boat to catch fish to augment the family larder. They keep all they catch, and they should.

But, one might ask, what of trout? One cannot expect a day's limit of trout to significantly supplement a family's meals, and, indeed, if one measured trout fishing in this wise there would almost always be an economic loss.

The British have a phrase for angling for species other than trout and salmon: coarse fishing. Snobbery in any form leaves me cold, but there is a germ of truth in this: Trout and salmon are special. Therein lies the rub for those of us who cherish those species. We want them to always be around, but many of us enjoy eating them.

My own love of fried or broiled brook trout goes back nearly fifty years, to a time when the ponds and streams I fished held native fish only. There were no rainbows or browns, as there are now, and the pressure on those waters was such that the trout population remained stable. Catching a mess of trout was as easy as gathering a bucket of oysters, and, as a child, I often accomplished both in one morning. Such fishing, alas, is as irretrievable as my youth, and I am perfectly willing to abide by today's rules.

My gripe is with those who regard the legally taken trout in my creel as a sign of moral degradation. I also feel sorry for those critics because they are missing a most important part of the angling ritual and might be likened to a man who has successfully wooed a lovely woman only to ignore her when the wedding ceremony is done.

It was inevitable that fly fishermen would be in the vanguard of the no-kill trend. They are, by and large, the most introspective, inquisitive, and disciplined of the anglers, and the nature of their sport lends itself to infinite and often tedious ramifications. Over the centuries, fly fishermen have created a literature that dwarfs that of any other form of angling, and entire texts have been written on the creation of a few new fly patterns. Many fly fishermen have an apparently insatiable appetite for detail, so much so, indeed, that some of them seem to have stopped angling altogether to devote all their spare time to tying flies or discussing new techniques.

Those who wish to embrace all the intricacies of fly-fishing are welcome to do so, but there are quite a few of us who engage in it with considerable success and only a modicum of special learning, who regard it as no more complicated than plugging for striped bass in the surf, or skindiving for conch.

All too often, from my point of view, a fascination with incredible and not always relevant minutiae has led fly fishermen too far from the basic quest: catching fish for food.

This is not to imply that taking fish isn't fun in itself, but only to suggest that much of the mystique surrounding catching trout on an artificial fly verges on the ludicrous. The mind that created magnificent symphonies and searing poetry and that split the atom has no proper adversary in a fish.

As I look back over a half-century of angling, there were innumerable occasions when the eating of the catch brought the endeavor to a proper close, not unlike the rhymed couplet at the close of a Shakespearian sonnet.

I think of the time when a friend and I hiked into a remote pond in New Hampshire in June, picking wild mushrooms on the way. Reaching the pond, we placed our mushrooms in the shade and went fishing. By early afternoon we had half a dozen big brook trout each, and six of them we kept alive on a quickly improvised stringer. We fried those fish, still twisting in the pan, over a little, quick-burning fire of dead hemlock, having first cooked some slab bacon and the mushrooms, which were set aside on a piece of birchbark to drain. It was a glorious repast, and—even allowing for the ambiance of our surroundings—it was then I became convinced that a just-caught trout has a more enticing flavor than one even a few hours dead.

Another of my best-remembered fish feasts took place at the foot of Musquarro Lake in Québec. The fish were *ouananiche,* or landlocked salmon, averaging about five pounds each. They were split down the back with backbone removed, then placed between two grills that were wired together. Brushed with melted butter, lemon juice, salt and pepper, and heavily dusted with brown sugar, they were cooked over an open fire. The cooking arrangement was capable of infinite variations of heat. Two men held the fish suspended above the fire by long loops of brass chain attached to the grills. Because the grills were wired together, it was possible to cook both sides of the fish without poking at them with a spatula.

What I am suggesting is that for many anglers denial of the eating ritual is a big mistake. But if you don't enjoy eating fish, or if you have no means of cooking them immediately, or properly keeping them until you reach a spot where they can be cooked, set them free. It is immoral to kill fish for the sole purpose of demonstrating your angling prowess, and almost as immoral to allow them to deteriorate to a state in which their original texture and flavor is lost.

There is even a way to enjoy eating a trout at streamside without the benefit of fire. Take paper-thin, cross-section slices from a fillet and marinate in lime or lemon juice, or a mixture of both, for half an hour and eat them with crackers, such as Saltines. This is an excellent way, perhaps with the addition of a good wine and a good cheese, to wile away a few hours at midday when the sun is glaring too brightly into your favorite pool.

It is also possible to cook a fish without the aid of a pot, pan, or grill. If, late at night on some boulder-strewn beach, you catch a striped bass, cut a thick, cross-section chunk from it, wrap it in a layer of rockweed, encase all in aluminum foil, and toss on the coals of a driftwood fire. Cooking time varies with the heat of the fire and the thickness of the weed covering and the piece of fish, so turn your fish after the first ten minutes and inspect at the end of twenty. A little salt and pepper can be used after cooking, but it really isn't necessary. (I rather suspect that many of our elaborate recipes for fish and game evolved from a time when much of it was nearly spoiled before it got to the kitchen, the spices being used to mask the unattractive flavor.)

And when you are devouring fish (even hallowed trout and salmon) rest assured that you are in good company.

About five hundred years ago, Dame Juliana Berners, Prioress of the nunnery of Sopwell near St. Albans in England, observed in her *Treatise on Fishing with an Angle:* "If in fysshing his sport fail him, the angler atte the leest hath his holsum walke and is mery at his ease, a swete ayre of the swete savor of the meed floures that makes him hungry; he heareth the melodyous armony of fowles; he seeth the young swannes, heerons, ducks, cotes and many other foules with theyr brodes . . . and if the angler take fysshe, surely, then, is there noo man merrier than he is in his apytyte."

God bless a merry appetite!

Scholarly readers might question whether "apytyte" in the quotation above carries the freight I have assigned it, and, indeed, in his 1930 translation into modern English of Dame Juliana's book, William Van Wyck renders the final lines: "If the angler happens to catch a fish, then surely no man is gladder in spirit than he." A check with Allan Gaylord, professor of English at Dartmouth College, however, reveals that while the original meaning of the word was not involved with an appetite for food, it was being so used by some writers as early as 1303.

The foregoing has been an attempt to point out that eating a fish does not imply a lack of reverence for it, and that in some instances a sense of reverence is enhanced by the act. It's such a simple equation. I love the

Catch and Release and Other Things

black duck and the Canada goose, but do not hesitate to shoot a few each year to eat. There is nothing insensitive about killing ducks, deer, geese, *or* fish if one follows through with proper respect for their once-living bodies and if one does all one can to protect them from overexploitation and their habitat from destruction or defilement.

Notes on Alaska

John Randolph

Notes on Alaska

September 1, 1979; Unalakleet, Alaska; 7:30 A.M.; 33 degrees, clear.

THERE was a frost last night, and the river is dropping finally after a flush of rain. Sandbars are beginning to appear—the places where the fisherman can stand and work the bends, riffles, and back-eddies. Silver salmon are in the river. It's the end of the run, and the fish are dying. The salmons—king, silver, chum, pink, sockeye—love the spots where the water breaks: the eddies, riffles, and still waters where they can find rest on the move upriver. The swim upstream on the Unalakleet is forty miles to the spawning grounds near Debauch Mountain. Each salmon will return to the gravel where it hatched from eggs laid down three to four years before its return to re-create.

The silvers lie in the small creeks where they enter the main Unalakleet. The silvers are pink sided or silver, depending on their time. When they come in fresh from the sea, they are gunmetal silver and they are called "bright fish," and the bright fish tarry a while just above Unalakleet village in the tidal estuary, where they prepare themselves for the fresh water. The preparation is sometimes full of showy acrobatics and seemingly madcap behavior. In the lower Unalakleet you see fish leaping, thrashing, and running madly across the surface. The fishing guides say the fish seek to rid themselves of sea lice in their running and jumping.

In any case, they must make the chemical changes necessary for life in fresh water. The water that gave them birth is strange on their return from the ocean, and the salmon must tarry in the saltwater-freshwater estuaries waiting for their bodies to adjust to the trip to home water.

The native people—Eskimos—have known for thousands of years that the salmon must stay for a while near the river mouths. There, at the great salmon-tarrying places, the Eskimos have made their living spots and have gone about their own self-perpetuation, living off the salmon runs that provide the food for winter.

The Eskimos set their nets along the Unalakleet River estuary, where the tides reach upriver and create the transition zone for the returning salmon. The Eskimos set the nets and return to harvest their loads of fish fresh from the sea. The fish are silver; their flesh is firm. The Eskimos fillet the fish on a sandy river bend and hang slabs of red meat to dry in the sun and the chill autumn air. Then the partially dried meat is moved to drying sheds behind the beach.

The fishing camps above the town are full of Eskimo life on weekends, when the river becomes a main thoroughfare for hunting and fishing natives. The boats—sixteen-foot, heavy-duty jobs with twenty- to fifty-horse outboards—zip up and down the river. The Eskimos race to camps at the headwaters of the Unalakleet, where they will hunt moose for winter meat. Then they return to the fishing camps where the drying salmon meat must be handled and moved and the nets emptied of their loads. The sound of outboard motors is everywhere.

When the Eskimos arrive at the fishing camps, there is much yapping, barking, and whining from the dog teams tied and left there during the trip upriver. The Eskimos, too, laugh, jabber, and giggle, and the whole meeting sounds like a Chinese fire drill. Eskimos—pure-blooded Eskimos—are clean-featured, beautiful, and happy oriental people. Their culture is endangered by an intruding world. Some young Eskimos are bitter.

We fish the estuaries beside the Eskimo fishing sheds, but no luck. Fly-fishing for silver salmon is tough business. My guide, whose name is Bob and who also owns the lodge I'm staying at, locates thirty to forty silvers in the Little North River, a ten-foot-wide, sluggish slough that runs into the North River. We ease up to the Little North and drive the bow of the boat onto the caving sandbanks at the slough's mouth.

"There are fish here. See the ripples on the surface?" Bob says.

The surface of the slough undulates with soft ripples, the play of large fish moving and swirling with their backs just below the surface. You can't see them in the muddy water, except when the pink flank of a huge fish colors the water here and there. I try Polaroids, but the sunlight is still too low and the damn things just turn everything dark. Slowly my eyes turn to the fish lying and milling in the pool. There, the indistinct form of a silver salmon, and another. Two pink silvers mill and play near the far bank.

I rig with a six-weight, sinking-tip line on a nine-foot Leonard Graphtek rod. I wonder as I rig if the rod can stand the pressure of these huge fish. These are Percherons. My little rods have never been tested as they will be tested now. I wonder about the knots—those damn blood knots of mine that never hold. This will be big-league pitching here in the little slough.

I cast over the big pool of silvers for thirty minutes before I realize that the fly—a bright, white, red-and-silver-tipped West Coast job—must be fed right to the fish. I've got to put the damn fly right in the brute's mouth. The fish is not thinking about food at this point. It can see dark at the end of the tunnel—it'll be gasping and dying in a few hours—it's get it off and die.

Bob is fly-casting to the fish, chucking the fly and line rather than casting. I figure he's probably fishing the brutes on fly for the first time for my benefit. After all, why should he make difficult what is easy on spinning gear?

"There he is," Bob says matter-of-factly, as though he'd hooked a carp. The fish jumps, heaving its ten pounds into the air, and then it thrashes and rolls heavily on the surface. The fight is over. I'm disappointed. So much weight and so little fight—so little zest for life. Perhaps it's all gone now. Perhaps there was more fight another, earlier day, several years ago, before it came in—or even thought of coming in—

from the ocean. But not now. The end is too close; the race is run. Why run another?

Lead is the thing. I can see it now: It's lead or no fish. I wrap on lead strips just above the fly, on the tippet that is no tippet, really, just a leader butt tied on as a tippet.

I cast up and let the white streamer drift back, sinking and creeping across the bottom in front of the fish's eyes. I can see the white fly as it creeps along in the clearing water. I can see the fish now—solid fish with their eyes on spawning and death. *Do they see the fly at all?* I ask myself. *Bite, you sonsabitches!* They slowly move aside. The fly interferes with their view of breeding and dying.

Casting—again, again, again. I become obsessed with the floating, sinking, crawling fly and the noses of the fish. My back aches from leaning toward the cast, toward the fly, toward the fish. Finally, I *think* the fish onto the fly. I think its mouth open. *Open, you stolid bastard! Open!* And its mouth closes on the white fly.

I can't see it happen, but I see the line slow for a second and I pull hard and feel the hook drive into something live and heavy. The silver fish thrashes ponderously to the surface and tries a leap—but no *Salmo salar* here, boys. It lurches back into the slough and the other fish scatter up and down the narrow channel. I horse and it horses. I look at the Graphtek rod arched in a full bow, waiting for the loud crack. It doesn't come. The fish flounders, and I horse it up on the bank and grab it in a vise-lock grip behind the tail and heave it up on the bank.

That's it, you egg-and-sperm machine! I mesmerized your eye, the one you focused on the spawning bed upriver.

I remove the hook from the mammoth hooked jaw and ease the fish into the water—launching a submarine. Its gill covers work slowly. It revives, gradually overcoming the build-up of lactic acid in its system. If I let go now, it'll turn over and drown. I hold its tail and ease the fish back and forth in the water. Its belly feels full and good in my hand. It swims sluggishly away. The other silver Percherons move aside and it rejoins them.

I watch Bob fish. It's business to him—you can see it in his face, in his casting. He's not after fish, he's after lodge business. "Fill the camp—sixteen people per week times one thousand dollars per week equals sixteen thousand dollars per week equals a profit of five thousand five hundred dollars less unusual expenses this week of broken water heater. Wonder if the weather will hold? Just the next two weeks is all we need. Will the water pump give out again tonight?" It's all in his face. And why not? The damn river runs full of horse-size salmon all summer, and fish can be a delight or a bore; it depends on where you've come from—New York City or Unalakleet.

We race downriver through the cold, arctic air to the lodge. Other fishermen are at the hand-carved wooden bar, sipping long drinks washed down with Earth, Wind, and Fire disco. Bob's feet start to go instinctively. He has another, catlike side that has no expression on the river. He tells me of his Force Recon Marine experiences in Vietnam. The accounts are straight—no hang-ups. I offer him *Dispatches* to read; he's genuinely interested.

September 2, 1979; Unalakleet, Alaska; noon; 32 degrees, clear; wind blowing in off Norton Sound.

It is said that the delicate arctic grayling is not selective, that it is a sucker for anything that floats. So, the feeling goes, the only thing to do is to fish for quantity and size. When you get tired of jockstrapping it fishing for salmon, just tie on any old dry fly and take grayling at will.

It didn't happen that way today. The grayling began to rise freely as we ate lunch on a sandbar in the North Branch of the Unalakleet River. We cleaned things up and crossed the river to a small island between a large backwater and a huge hole in the main current.

I tied on a Royal Wulff and cast nonchalantly to the rising fish while the guides slung hardware. The *splup, splup, splup* of free-rising grayling continued, but the fish were not interested in the Wulff pattern. A natural fly floated by within reach, and I picked it gently from the water and looked it over carefully. It had the look of a mayfly—some kind of Alaskan mayfly with a pale, blue-green color.

I found something similar in my fly box, tied it on, and offered it with anticipation. The fly floated long and drag-free in the slick near the edge of the current where the fish continued their rhythmic rising. It appeared to be a perfect float, but the grayling inexplicably would not fulfill their reputation for indiscriminate gluttony. The thought that I was actually striking out on grayling was unnerving, and I cast again and again with increasing determination. To no avail. The grayling would not be stupid, although the dry-fly pattern I used seemed to be a near-perfect imitation of the hatch.

On the next cast I delivered a straight, tight line and leader, and then tugged the fly down into the surface film. There followed a live tug and an exciting fight—but almost delicate after the muscular salmon I had been catching earlier. The grayling were not taking duns, but were feeding on emergers just beneath the surface film. After that, the grayling came to the fly on every cast, until fifteen minutes later when the hatch ceased and the river was quiet and slick and seemingly empty without the dimples of rising grayling. *Grayling can be selective*, I thought, as we left the large pool at the North Branch of the Unalakleet.

September 3, 1979; Unalakleet, Alaska; 8 P.M.; 32 degrees, clear.

Behind the hewn-log lodge that the guides have fashioned with chainsaws, and set above the river, is an arctic hill. I want to see the river and the tundra stretching away to the Bering Sea. I trudge uphill, my breath catching in my chest. The sun drops slowly, but the light is right for color and I don't mind the camera on its strap around my neck. The light is low and angular and it sends shadows out from the riverbanks and hills; the pictures will be good.

I look back over the roof of the lodge and along the river toward the ocean. I can see the big Bering Sea shining brightly below a long cloud line. To the south, the tundra opens into a brown-carpeted valley that stretches to low mountains. I watch the valley for a long time, searching its curves and rolls and sinuous lakes for the pleasure the roaming gives my eyes.

The road to the hilltop is one set of tire tracks on the muskeg tundra. Near the hilltop I come upon a tube stuck in the ground. The top is in brass and it says, "Unlawful to Disturb. U. S. Dept. of Interior." Heavy stuff here in wilderness Alaska.

A few yards farther on I see another sign that states less presumptuously—this one is hand painted and on wood—"Henrietta Wilson native allotment." Henrietta has been given fifty acres by a munificent U. S. of A. Fifty acres is her hunk of a homeland so vast that the caribou travel three thousand miles between summer and winter ranges. Henrietta Eskimo—daughter of a man who knew no property lines, a man who felt the seasons come and go as easily as the wind, who took the swarming fishes, who hunted the caribou with the wolves across three million fenceless acres, who heard no machine sound, who called everything his within sight of this hilltop and beyond—now "owns" fifty acres with all the blueberries she can pick from it. Thank you, Uncle Sam!

I look at Henrietta's sign—hand painted and with no mention of the U. S. Dept. of Interior. Behind the sign, about two miles distant, rises a Stonehenge, an apparition come true on the top of an Alaskan hilltop. The man-made towers look like rock monoliths, black in the late-evening sun. They rise in sinister angularity like a set for some Kubrick movie.

Where do they face, these radar eyes and ears of the Dewline Defense? I ask myself. Northwest, it appears. Is this the direction, then, that the cunning strategists felt the giant sneak attack of Armageddon would come from? The Ruskies's machines would hurtle across the top of the globe, across the Bering.

Waters Swift and Still

But thanks to these towers, with the men at their scopes tracing blips of light through the arctic winter nights, with the eternal aurora borealis showering above them, we would be safe in New York. Henrietta's fifty acres, too, would be safe.

The station is an empty shell now, and the Eskimos have blown the locks off the doors and found play inside—great place for a drunk, among the obsolete circuited radar and the wheeled vehicles left in their stalls. Who can steal them? There are no roads beyond the base fences.

I look to the northwest across the long, brown, tundra valleys to the coastal hills. *There!* Another hilltop base, another watch-and-listen station. *Have I been here before?*

I think back. *Where was it? Where? . . . Thessaloniki, Greece—1965. Yes. There, on a Marine NATO landing for the King of Greece, who almost killed some dumb Marine while driving to the landing show in his Maserati. There, near the Bulgarian border on the coast where Alexander crossed and took Persia. There, the watchtowers of an empire—great, round towers of stone laid up on each promontory; the sentries could see the next tower and light the signals of warning when enemy ships were sighted. There, in Stonehenge, Greece, Henrietta Atexalopolis's fifty acres were safe—almost.*

A dog salmon thrashed in a Unalakleet River back-eddy, dying.

September 4, 1979; Kulik River, Alaska; 7 A.M.; 30 degrees, clear.

The Kulik River is full of red sockeye salmon as we fly into camp. You can see them from the bushplane as we make the circle to land, banking above the river behind the camp. The sockeye are spaced evenly in the river, and they are dark red and make the blue water of the river look like a sinuous checkerboard.

We bank and come in fast and taxi up to the sand beach in front of the cabins set snug against a south-facing hill on the north end of Nonvianek Lake. Behind the hill are mountain crags and rolling upland tundra. The air is autumn clear, and the flinty crags and tundra valleys remind me of a Montana autumn. We are in the river of sockeye an hour later.

On this September day the sockeye are home from the sea and in their final, most desperate act. A million sockeye lie spawning in the mile of river between Kulik and Nonvianek lakes. A million fish evenly spaced along the river in breeding schools. I watch them, fighting, dropping eggs, digging redds, angrily chasing competition. The males, with their mouth parts hooking into a kype more and more each day, are fiercely beautiful.

I wade upstream through a river of blue, among thousands of red-backed, darting, thrashing, digging fish. When I approach they flee in schools and then return quickly to their spawning and fighting. The males run at each other and thrash on the surface. In the backwaters, spent and dying sockeye thrash and roll spasmodically. Dead sockeye lie rotting along the shorelines, and fish stench overwhelms the air and water. Spawning and death spasms surround and emerse me. I feel taken down into the water by it and become part of a birth-death orgasm.

Fly-fishing seems an effete act in such a setting, but I fish and immediately snag one of the thrashing sockeye, *not* my quarry. I want the rainbows that lie obscured between the sockeye, feeding on the spawn as it exudes from the fecund females. The river runs full of spawn, a great milkshake fresh from a natural blender. The rainbows lie behind the sockeye and dart here and there through the spawners—gray destroyers moving swiftly through a large convoy of heavy ships. The rainbows snap up the drifting eggs. The sockeye chase them unsuccessfully; the rainbows are too fast. They are fat rainbows, much heavier than the swift-water rainbows I have known in the rivers of New England. Spawn-full are these rainbows, gorging themselves before the lean months of winter.

I can't get to the rainbows for the sockeye. I'm fishing in a fisherman's paradise, but there are too many fish. I keep hooking the sockeye on the swing. The rainbows are there, but the sockeye are bigger and more numerous. I hook one, play it in after fifteen minutes of workhorse tug-of-war, and release it. I'm into the dorsal fin of another sockeye immediately. Finally, I rip the fly off and stomp to the bank to reconnoiter and regroup.

The still water at the bank sickens me. Rotting sockeye pave the cobblestones. It's impossible to walk without stepping on—and into—rotting fish, fetid fish. When I step on the rotted, soft flesh of a salmon lying in two feet of water, the mushy feeling shoots up my leg. I peer down through the water at the fish turned thing. It is covered with a fuzzlike decay. The sockeye's color has disappeared. The fuzz is tan-gray; it covers the fish's entire body—eyes, fins, tail. The decaying fish defines decay, the rapid natural conversion of fish flesh to another form. I know I will always see this fish when I hear or read of decay. It joins the sight of maggot masses squirming on a sheep's flanks on a hot summer New England pasture day in my pantheon of flesh-decay horrors.

The rocks are covered with salmon paté. Salmon rotted and transmuted to this smelly sockeye paté have turned the still-water edges of the river into a putrid, greased-cobblestone horror. I slip and slide to the riverbank, sure that I will fall face-first into the rotting fish. I feel my face sinking into the soft fuzz of a rotting salmon, my hands grasping at paté-covered rocks.

You do not sit on the banks of a sockeye spawning stream during these final days. Dead salmon, sockeye paté, the intoxicating stench, and bear crap declare: "Fisherman, don't sit here!"

The bear crap is especially disturbing—great piles of it here and there, filled with undigested salmon eggs. But the trodden-down grass is more disturbing, and the tracks strike terror in the most placid soul. Mammoth tracks in the mud along the banks are huger than you have ever seen tracks be. These tracks and their makers are the biggest damn things in your life; the makers have claws and huge teeth. They are brown bears with implacable stares and poor eyesight; they dislike other bears competing with them for their fishing territories. You walk upright and look about the size of a small bear. Walking on the bears's paths in the high grass along the bank will be very, very dangerous. I think of these things

Notes on Alaska

on the bank, trying to ponder how to catch rainbows. I decide to leave the riverbank where the bears travel for the safety of the river. The river is safer, yes, much safer than the tall grass where the bears travel and can't see you until you meet them face-to-face.

One guide who seems to know about the bears confirms that they cannot see well. They don't like humans, he says, but they don't fear them, except where humans are allowed to hunt them. Where they can be hunted, the bears will flee, trampling trees, shrubs, and flowers to leave the gunshot vicinity of humans. But here on Kulik, no hunting is allowed, and the bears have no fear, which is more reason for fishermen to fear the unexpected encounter. The unexpected with brown bears is always to be avoided. The bear-expert guide taps his shoulder-holstered .44 magnum. "Necessary equipment around here," he says, and does not elaborate. Later I learn that he has been charged by a large brown bear at his camp on the river. The bear charged, and he killed it with a lucky shot. He knows he was lucky in that one spinal-system shot, the only shot that would have stopped the bear before it was on him.

He is still nervous about the attack two days later. When I ask him about his stand with a pistol against the charging bear, he gives me stoic advice: "If you're going to carry one of these pistolas, you'd better file the front sight blade down smooth. You'll only have time for one shot on a charging bear, and when you miss, he'll shove the pistol up your ass. It'll go a lot easier if the sight blade's gone."

All the mealtime discussions from now on turn to bear stories. The bears are on the guests' and guides' minds subliminally—a presence that becomes terribly heavy and oppressive as darkness falls along a river camp and you scurry to do things before nightfall. A bear roars a visceral, barrel-chested declaration. You realize as you open your sleeping bag in your tent that you are merely a naked intruder in the bear's land. Let it fish. Stay to the center of the river where you can see its approach. Give the bear its paths and high grass, where it will eat dying salmon and lie taking long naps and blowing long, brown-bear sighs in the steaming grasses. Give it that and stay away from its path.

The brown-bear-understanding guide says a bear will false charge

Waters Swift and Still

with its ears pricked. It'll charge at you to within thirty yards and then stop for a better look. It may stand up on its hind legs and look at you then, and if it does it will look like a curious boy trying to peer over a fence. If he drops his ears, watch out!

I wade back into the Kulik River after rainbows, through the salmon paté and the floating dead fuzzies to the swift, deep runs where I know the rainbows will be.

I choose the head of a fast, dark run beside a cut bank, and begin to work down through the heavy water. The wading is dangerous, and my felt-soled wader boots continually break loose. I cast upstream toward the bank and mend upstream so the line will sink and the fly will tick bottom as it reaches me. I want the fly to tick bottom and then swing by me and rise. The rainbows will spot the rising egg pattern and dash to grab it before the current carries it away.

I watch the line where the orange sinking-tip meets the yellow of the line belly, and I see the line jerk forward and feel the jolt of a hard strike in my arm and shoulder at the same instant. There is a violent tugging on the line and rod, and a rainbow shoots out of the water, shakes, dances across the white-water stretch below the cut bank, and disappears, running back and forth through the dashing, red sockeye.

When I have subdued it but not finished it, I bring the gunmetal-bright rainbow up and hold it under its belly and release the fly from its jaw. I hold the fish under the belly for a while, sliding it back and forth in the water gently until its movements quicken. Suddenly the fish is gone.

I hear a swishing sound behind and above me on the streambank. Eight feet away a huge brown bear peers at me, its ears pricked and its face showing that implacable stare that says: "There is nothing at the center of this world but me." I watch the ears as I back slowly into the current, away from the bank and the bear and into the ranks of spawning sockeye. The stench of death is on the river, but I do not smell it.

Notes on Alaska

September 5, 1979; Brooks River, Alaska; 8 A.M.; 33 degrees, clear.

If you're an angler you have two good friends here: your guide and your eyes equipped with Polaroid glasses. If your guide happens to be Steve Rajeff, six-time United States fly-casting champion, you have an edge. Our first clue that the day would be good came as we flew over the river before landing.

"See the rainbows lying along the inside bend of the river?" our pilot asked as we circled in a tight, banking move that tipped the plane precariously on its left wing. We could see distinctly the red sockeye lying to the outside of the bend, and we could discern other fish lying all along the shallow water at the inside of the bend, as though in military formation. The fishermen who worked the river below us obviously did not know where the rainbows were, because they were fishing in the wrong places. The fish were lying at the inside of the river, but the fishermen were all fishing the fast water to the outside of the bend.

Rajeff and the pilot had a good-natured laugh over the fishermen far below, but the rest of us laughed uneasily. We knew that without the guide and the pilot, we also would be just ignorant sports lost on strange water. We flew to the lake where the river entered, landed, and walked quickly upstream to begin fishing. Rajeff took one rainbow after another, and after a short while, a fisherman who apparently couldn't take the demonstration any longer without explanation sidled up to me and inquired: "Hey, what's going on here, a class in fly-fishing? Who's that guy, anyway?"

"He's our guide," I said. "He could see as we came in on the plane that the rainbows were lying in the shallow water. He's very good."

Rajeff showed us how to spot the rainbows—the gray slivers of light in the bright water—and he explained how to make the cast. We caught rainbows, but not at will the way he did. It was like bonefishing, except the rainbows did not cruise the way bonefish do. I spotted the large slivers of gray, cast to them, and watched the pink egg pattern until it paused. When I struck, the rainbows would run hard and scatter all the other fish.

Waters Swift and Still

Later, as we worked our way back downriver to the plane, we stopped to photograph a she bear and her cub fishing for sockeye. The mother stood on her hind legs, chest deep in a long slick, and scooped spent sockeye as they drifted downstream toward the lake. We could hear the chilling crunch of bones as she crushed the skull of a fish. Then she'd carry the limp carcass in her mouth to the streambank where her cub waited, sitting patiently on its haunches.

Suddenly behind us in the grass there was a long, incredibly deep sigh. It was a sigh of opulent, unrestrained, well-fed contentment from a mammoth chest, and it had so much lapdog quality in it that Rajeff and I looked at each other and giggled—nervously.

September 6, 1979; Alagnak River, Alaska; 6 A.M.; 20 degrees, heavy frost, clear.

We are joined at breakfast by two spike-camp fishing guides. We camped near a fishing shack, and we had heard them digging their way upriver during the night, their outboard-motor propellers hitting the gravel bars as they sought and missed the channels in the darkness. They drank coffee with us, but would not share in breakfast. We were telling fishing stories when another motor buzzed on the river, and the fishing-shack owner turned into the river-bend backwater and tied up at the sandy cut bank below the shack. We were uneasy about being caught camping on his native allotment of land; no one knew how he would take the intrusion. I'd heard stories from Ernie Schwiebert about nasty occurrences—encounters between whites and native Americans on Kodiak Island.

He was an Eskimo and he had his wife with him. In repose, their faces carried weathered, wrinkled smiles—the mark of the Eskimo's good-natured, giggle response to outrageous natural hardships. We talked too much, perhaps to show we were good whites and not interlopers or White Men. Once we felt at ease in the warmth of his reception, however, we began to ask him the questions we all had in mind, never having seen an Eskimo at such close range.

What did he use this corrugated-tin cabin for? Fishing and winter trapping, he said. Then he wanted to know if we'd come up from San Francisco or Los Angeles. He said he liked those cities and visited them often. But he said he preferred Las Vegas. He liked to go there and gamble. He wanted to know if I liked gambling at Las Vegas, but I said I'd never been there—couldn't afford it. I also had to admit I'd never seen Los Angeles. I shifted a little from leg to leg, and had the uncomfortable feeling that I'd been about to patronize a man who'd already made the Grand Tour. Things are not what they seem here in Alaska. He told us where to fish for the big ones.

City Angler

Nick Lyons

City Angler

HERE AND THERE the stony city allows us to see water: fountains in front of office buildings, a muddy lake, a clear but fenced-in reservoir, the East River and the Hudson River, their flows heavy and silty and brown. My eye, drawn always to water, misses none of it—not even the huge pool that forms on the northeast corner of Eighty-fourth Street and West End Avenue after a great rain, the stream coursing down from Broadway, the runs, riffles, and eddies of a mighty trout river in miniature, in sad parody.

Water in the city can be farcical, sentimental. It is a joke. It is the flag of thwarted longings. And it can evoke that easy dichotomy between city and country, for water is out of character here and only exists to imp its free and wild counterpart.

"I am exactly where I want to be," says my friend Russell Chatham, "not at all by chance." He lives in Deep Creek, Montana, near the Yellowstone and the spring creeks, not far from the Boulder River. And he writes there and paints and fly-fishes. *I* would seem to be exactly where I do not want to be, not at all by chance.

There are reasons; there *always* are reasons.

Family or finances, social links and fears and future promises: There are always reasons.

But the inescapable facts are that I am drawn to the woods and waters and I loathe this gray city in which I live and have almost always lived, counting its threats to all I value with nicest relish.

Be fair: There are compensations. This apartment in which I write is an amiable place—a bit small, without a view, but a home now; my children have found their paths through the undergrowth of this city and touch its energy and excitement; my wife breathes better in museums and has a community of painters who, next to her canvases themselves, are her lifeblood. "Knock on the door of the provinces," she says, "and what do you find?" I dread to ask. So be it. That's not what I've found afield, where I breathe better.

For me the city has bred a certain tension. It has, in what I have written about trout fishing, led to self-irony—a depiction of the inevitable mishaps and misadventures, of frustrations that make amusing tales but that, below the skin, sere the soul. For you cannot take a sport as complex and precise as fly-fishing for trout and allocate it a day here and a day there; you cannot pinch it and cheat it so. Then the long trip out to the East Branch is cramped into space that will not hold it, and the hand goes wild and the full force of the weather and water's vagaries play on you. In short, you become a fumbling idiot.

This makes funny stories and a weary heart.

But there is a corollary.

William Humphrey speaks of those who make a passion of their pastime, forgetting priorities. Trout fishing is not an art or an occupation; it is a pastime.

"I love trout fishing, Nick," says my friend Thom Green, an oil geologist, "but I'd rather hunt for oil."

This little truth will be axiomatic to the man who truly loves his work, whatever it is, or to the artist, for whom it would never be otherwise, and it will be heresy to the fanatic who would say, "All for trout or the world well lost." Theodore Gordon lost the world, weaving in his isolation a fabric of dreams for a thousand men born too late or with too little—or with more horse sense or more conscience. I do not think we are here only to fly-fish for trout. But I have had that longing—to be alone, intensely engaged in my pastime, making it a passion. Now and again, when the only sloughs I fish are those of despond, when the full weight of this gray place creeps into the last nerve of my body, I have dreamed of bolting to a greener place. Permanently. I have dreamed of "annihilating all that's made/To a green thought in a green shade," losing myself in the sweet mysteries and pleasures of a pursuit that sometimes seems as purposeful and moral and proper as anything I do in this odd vale of perplexities.

Sometimes I have dreamed of taking my work to my pastime. But there is a dour lesson in "Two Fishermen," Morley Callaghan's rueful story about an amiable man who took the job that would enable him to travel about in the provinces a bit and manage some fine days fishing: He became an itinerant hangman.

Chatham, of course, hangs no one.

And the Chatham Factor, which I admire, may yet claim me.

But not quite yet.

There is a literary figure of speech called the oxymoron; it has nothing to do with being an idiot, though some people surely think that holding two opposing ideas in your head at once qualifies you for idiocy. Thus, Richard Crashaw's "sweetly killing dart" and "deaths shall live" are oxymoronic, and so is John Donne's "imprison me, for I/Except you enthrall me, never shall be free." Thus, too, in a considerably lesser key, is Lyons and the city an oxymoron.

It is an abrupt paradox.

But the oxymoron, because of its inherent power, is much more interesting than, say, the lyric description of a sunset, all pretty and patchy and purple. The oxymoron has pith and energy. Spice. Resonance. It is not a valentine, sickly sweet with sentimentality. An oxymoron incorporates the opposites in the world, which are always there. You cannot escape them, as Chatham well knows, even in Deep Creek, Montana.

But I do not remain in the city because of the unique aesthetic advantage it might give me. No one in his right mind seeks pain; in its own good time pain will find you. I live in the city for "reasons," the deepest of which I shouldn't and won't tell here—or anywhere. I live here now, at this moment in my life.

Fishing is no less a part of my life because I do it only occasionally at this point in my life. There have been several blocks of time, cut from the gray cities of my mind, in which I have had fishing available to me every waking hour for a week, two weeks, a month, an entire summer—on the Big Hole, the Grimsá, on Henrys Lake, in the Catskills. Nor was I then always prone to my usual disasters. A day or two of conscientious casting and the line went were it should go—most of the time. Four or five good salmon on my line and I knew to the ounce how much I could pressure them, and lost none. I did not always fish those days, but I was glad it was there, available—very early in the morning, before the sun broke, at dusk, and late at night. And I loved that measurable increase in skill of which I found myself capable.

Yet sometimes, when I have fished intensely for a day or a week, day after day, enjoying myself into utter exhaustion—until my eyes glazed and sun sores sprouted on my casting hand—I did not want it to end, but I was elated when it was over. "If all the year were holidays," I console myself, "to sport would be as tedious as to work." But then I remind myself that fishing has never been a *holiday* for me at all: It has, even in the midst of my busiest city days, a curious hold on me; it is part of me, and I do not ever really separate those days on the water from those off.

I do not like fishing less because I sometimes like a trip to be done. There are other days, other things I must do: Soon enough the flame will rise up again. I have met "professional" fishermen who seemed to me to have had quite their full fill of it. I'm in no particular hurry for that to happen, but I'd like—oh, surely—to fly-fish more. And I'd like more in my life of those things that make fly-fishing more than to fish. I love the places in which the thing is practiced. I love old cabins and rotting docks and marshes and sloughs and dirt trails and no trails and the elusive, varied, intensely exciting life of rivers. I love to have opened the door and shut it behind me and to be fully in a world where only that shy brown at the tail of the Willow Pool matters. I love to have hunted him, drawn him to my fly, perhaps hooked and netted him. And I love the memories of these things. And I love the equipment stored in my fish closet—the emblems of the sport, the rods and reels, the boxes of flies, the waders that still carry the caked mud and odor of some last-fished river into the gray city winter.

My friend Robbie, who does not fish, who has seen me in some ferocious moods, tells me: "Nick, you should fish more. You don't know how elated your face looks when you merely *talk* of it."

Don't I?

Sometimes, here in the city, I think of the variety of people out there in the provinces who fish: dry-fly purist, big-game troller, plug-caster, spinner, cane-poler, bait fisherman; I think of the users of kites and teasers, frog harnesses, five-inch plugs, dough balls, size 22 imitations of midge pupae; I think of those who fish for salmon, trout, tarpon, bass, muskie, flounder, bluegill, bluefish, walleye, perch. It is a vast army that marches out to fish, a vast array. And they often seem not only to have little in common but to be members of differing—even warring—tribes.

I have been, at one time or another, a fisher of all those persuasions. I gigged my first trout and could happily end my days fishing poppers for bluegill on an Oklahoma pond. I have already been known to catch chub. Fishing less than I'd like, I became more interested in the quality of my fishing, the nature of the pursuit, than in fishing itself. Foraging out in the provinces, I have tried all types of fishing but prefer the fly rod, which demands most and which deepens in every way the fishing experience. I like it most and fish it most often, but not exclusively.

Everywhere there are links, and often I find them off the water. My friend Michael Di Simone, who runs a restaurant, loves sharks and bluefish and stripers, and he often catches them on rods I could use as wading staffs. But when we talk—often on the gray pavements of upper Broadway—an excitement enters our voices, tale leads to tale, time vanishes, and we are of one stripe.

What links all fishermen, wherever they live and whatever they fish for, is not their degree of skill or the fact that they are equally adept at all the angling persuasions. What measures them is not necessarily the contests or the tournaments they've won, the trophies they've taken, or even the amount of time they have spent fishing; the tournaments, I fear, only spoil the barrel. The connection and the measure of the men lies in the spirit with which they fish or carry fishing inside them. Michael's tales are no less engaging to me than mine are to him.

Certainly competence is part of the game, or we'd be talking about fumblers not fishermen. But skill is the instrument in angling that permits us to practice the sport more pleasurably: It is not an end in itself.

There is such a sweetness to the act itself, especially in fly-fishing, that I am struck by a deep sadness whenever I hear all the backbiting and gossip, when I see the peacocking and bravado, when I see good fun metamorphosed into bad blood.

Here in the city I am too often too much in a heat to do any kind of fishing to understand how anyone could be so foolish as to allow it to become for him something sick and strange.

Chatham, whose angling is part of the fabric of his life, for whom it is an inseparable fact and pleasure, would not let it become such. Fishing *can* be so entwined with a life: in the provinces or in the metropolises. And if we let it, it will make our lives a bit richer, sprinkled bright with the rich colors of the flies we use or the game we pursue or the inexpressibly lovely places in which we pursue them.

City Angler

Not long ago I met a guy named George whom I had not seen in nearly thirty years. We had played half-court basketball together on cement courts in the heart of the city when we were kids. We had both been fiercely competitive in those days, full of the fire of this city game. The tough, competitive spirit had served him well. He was president of a corporation, he told me, making (he told me) "mid-six figures," and there was shark in his eyes. He was tight—a taut predator of high finance. I knew what he needed immediately.

"You ought to fish more," I told him.

"How can *you* fish," he asked me, "when you're not even making a living?"

Now and again, dreaming, I would like to be a captain of industry, able to charter a flight on two days' notice to catch the green drake hatch on the Henrys Fork; now and again, I would like to have the wherewithal to fish Patagonia, New Zealand, Yugoslavia; I have been bitten by salmon and would love a spare five grand for a week this July on one of the choicer salmon routes. I know several captains of industry who have retained the human measure George lost and who fish with quite the passion we poor folk think is our exclusive treasure. Money and the "true passion" ain't mutually exclusive. It's the balance and the proportion that count. The sensible man does not sacrifice a profession for a pastime but earns well to sport well—and then he allows the virtues of the pastime to color his working life.

But I am not very sensible and scarcely very sharkish; I like to make things—like books—but I am quite indifferent to that edge that drives men to make more and more money. The balance is wrong. My fly-fishing life is always there, nudging me, winding its way, like a fugue, through everything I do. It brushes my imagination with hopes and memories and dreams; it draws my restless hand into its crafts of tackle-tinkering; even its names—Hendrickson, Madison, Blue Quill, Blue

Waters Swift and Still

Charm, Rusty Rat, Henrys Fork, Beaverkill, Battenkill, Payne, Hardy—are cleansing, concrete, and distracting. Its trips, far and near, are bright moments cut from the engulfing gray. They are real, my business life is often illusory (my accountant uses harsher terms). Surely I have suffered enough from lack of money to know it is real. It simply does not feel so. It has no affection, no heart. Neither it nor the making of it has the feel of a wild trout, the rhythm of a river, the magic of a bamboo rod about it. Thom would rather hunt for oil, but I suspect it is the hunting, the engagement of his mind and spirit with the activity, that captures him most.

Fishermen are often like that: preferring the concrete to the abstract. In the city, the abstraction of money is the medium of exchange: Loving to fish, loving the appurtenances of fishing, helps me—in my practical life—not much at all.

We are not one thing, unchanging, for all time. We are, perhaps, as George Herbert says, "twentie sev'rall men each sev'rall houre." We exist in time as well as in place: What we are at one period is not what we would always be. I may yet seek a better set of terms with the Chatham Factor.

But right now I work and live in cities and I fish. I love rivers and fly-fishing and I remain in this gray city. For now. The balance is tenuous. When I am lucky, I enjoy my work and take my rivers when I can get them. Sometimes, with too little river in my veins, I feel I would dry up, go mad, bolt. I look for water in the city. I pause at the river on Eighty-fourth Street and West End Avenue, which is farcical, sentimental. I try to balance the abrupt paradox of my life.

I teeter.

But I am satisfied.

For now.

Home Waters

Charles Gaines

Home Waters

UNTIL I was out of college and married, my father and I rarely got along anywhere but in a fishing boat. Mostly it was my fault that we didn't get along. I was not an easy kid to raise, particularly for a man who was almost forty when I was born, a perfectionist who was forced to spend his middle years wrestling both with himself and certain members of the family he had married into. He felt, therefore (understandably, it seems now), a little chapped about having gotten for an only son a kid who needed wrestling, too.

My father was, back then, a gentleman of strenuous and often debilitating appetites. In his forties he nearly died from a bleeding ulcer he got from the IRS and too much rich food. His own father had died the color of a peach from booze, and he would have, too, had he not, sometime in his fifties, finally won his twenty-year-long struggle with that particular appetite.

His appetite for money and professional success, though in the end it got him most of what he wanted, was soured for a long time by the frustrations of putting his good mind and MIT engineering degree to work within the stodgy, hierarchical family business he married into. Now that he is almost eighty, his appetites run mostly to electric sheets, tennis, Hawaiian Punch, warm weather, Belgian loafers, and travel;

about the only hunger he has in common with himself at fifty, or forty, or twenty, is for fishing—the one thing he could never get enough of in middle age that didn't disagree with him.

He started me fishing, for channel bass around the jetties at Mayport, Florida, before I was five, and he taught me to fly-fish before I was ten. By then we had moved from Florida to Birmingham, Alabama, and he was in full swing wearing himself thin. He fished with buddies all over the world back then, for various reasons. At home, in home waters, I think he fished mostly to recover; for that, and to give himself and me time to get along.

I'd be in trouble in school, say, or Bobby Carlson and Frank Young and I would have been seen running naked down the Mountain Brook Parkway or caught shooting street lamps with BB guns. He'd come home from the office, sit in his lounge chair in front of the TV and hear about it, still dressed in his suit pants and a button-down Brooks Brothers shirt, still looking avid from the day but worn down by it, too. He'd sit and ponder whatever it was I had done, then get suddenly crisp around the mouth. My mother would ask that "it" wait until after dinner, which was served every evening at six-fifteen on the dot by a black man and woman with whom I was on much more intimate terms than I was with my father. "It" came about eight-thirty or nine and consisted usually of a half-dozen measured strokes to my butt with a two-foot-long shoehorn. It never occurred to me then that my father was often spanking more than me—I believed then, and do now, that I usually deserved what I got—and therefore I didn't understand until much later the gesture that sometimes followed the spankings. I'd be in bed, maybe asleep. He'd open the door to my room and stand there for a minute, backlit by the hall.

"Son?" he'd say. He'd walk into the room, sit on the side of my bed, and bend over and hug me, smelling like scotch. Then, if it was spring or summer or fall, my father would say, "We'll go fishing on Saturday."

The first home water I remember was at Louis Ford's ranch on the Black Warrior River near Tuscaloosa. Louis had for fishing water not only the river but a number of ponds and lakes full of bass, crappie, and big bluegill. We'd fish the lakes on the surface in the morning and late afternoon for bass, using Dalton Specials and a lure Louis said imitated a baby bird fallen out of a nest. In the middle of the day my father and I would take sardines and crackers and RC Colas down the slow, muddy river and fill the boat with crappie and bluegill. Sometimes Louis would go with us on the river and tell stories while he fished—like about the time my father kept the boat from sinking, probably saving their lives, when a stump tore a hole in the bow in high water and my father patched it on the spot with a raincoat and screws he took out of an old wooden tackle box.

Louis was a big, red-faced, horn-handed countryman and he and my father loved each other. One winter my father invited Louis up to a formal dance at a country club in Birmingham. Somehow, dressed in an unfamiliar tuxedo, Louis got his feelings hurt at the dance and drove himself and his beautiful wife home to Tuscaloosa. He and my father didn't see much of each other after that night. Louis died years later without either of them having put a patch to whatever happened at the party.

For a few years after Louis's place, our home water was a series of private bass lakes around Birmingham that belonged to friends and business associates of my father. Some of those lakes were prettier or fishier than others, but every one of them gave my father pleasure and calm. If it were a weekday during the summer, he would come home from the office around two and we would fish until dark; if it were Saturday or Sunday we would fish all day. Before we actually got to the lake—on the car ride out or during the meticulous preparations we made together— he could be thinking about things and irritable, his painstaking reaction to stress shunted for the time being into worrying the tackle, electric motor, batteries, and raingear together; into wondering if I had on enough clothes or had been to the bathroom. But once we reached the lake and he opened the door to one of his succession of yachtlike Buicks, stepped out, and looked at the water, he quit wrestling anything. It was time out for him, and he would come open like a fist unclenching. I could have broken into his liquor cabinet the night before, stolen a car and driven through the lobby of the Alabama Theater, and all he'd have to say about it beside a bass lake the next day—grinning hungrily, grabbing the rods and the tackle box, and leaving me to bring the motor and batteries down—would be: "Come on, Skip. You don't catch fish with your line out of water."

It didn't matter whether we caught fish or not, though we usually did. He'd sit in the back running the electric motor, both of us fly-fishing a bank with yellow poppers, and have a party—yelling at every hit, chuckling while he fought a fish, and bitching when he missed one, telling me whenever my popper drifted into his water to "Dammit, cast in *front* of the boat," pointing out beaver signs and wild fruit trees, teaching me how to smell a bream bed and to tell in my sinuses when low pressure was coming. And he'd be talking nonstop about Crunch and Des stories, John Alden Knight, his youth, his voice so detached and unemphatic and continuous that you had the impression he was not so much talking as just scoring his fishing.

When I was fifteen my father bought his own lake near a place called Margaret, about forty-five minutes from Birmingham. Lake Tadpole, as he named it, has been home water to him ever since, and it was to me until I married and left Alabama. Tadpole is really two lakes, a small upper one and a twenty-two-acre lower one, set in a valley in the north Alabama hills. It is a beautiful place—the big lake a buxom, feminine shape ringed by dogwoods and fruit trees and old pines—and he and I believe it is as good a piece of bass water as there is in Alabama. But its real significance to me is as the place my father and I went to get along after I ran away from one prep school and was kicked out of another, after his mother died, after I left college and hitchhiked around the country for a year working on mackerel boats and mango farms, and after—finally realizing I would never come to work for it—he sold the division of the family company that he had built from scratch.

We still go there to get along, though getting along anywhere is easier now. We go out of habit, I suppose. We still like the perspective that being at the lake together in a fishing boat gives each of us on the other—the depth-of-field of hundreds of old afternoons of leniency with each other that it provides.

I had Lough Corrib in Ireland for home water for two years, and didn't fish in Georgia. Dick Wentz and I shared a piece of fine home water called Rath's Pond in Iowa for a couple of years, then we both moved to Wisconsin and had a triangle of Lake Michigan and the creeks in Door County for three more. During those years my wife and I quickly had three children and got easy graduate degrees. I made a living having fun, published a few stories and poems, and fished around in British Columbia and the Gaspé, in the Keys and the Bahamas, in Mexico and Cozumel and the Yucatán. There was hardly anything to recover from during those seven years. Everybody got along beautifully and it wasn't ever necessary to take bearings in order to get from one place to another. Home water, therefore, good as it was sometimes, didn't mean too much. In one gorgeous, fir-lined home creek in Door County—near the mouth of which Wentz and I, and only Wentz and I, would take perfectly colored two-pound brookies every September on deer-hair dry flies—I even rigged a fishing picture for a magazine. I hooked a long-dead, ten-pound Lake Michigan steelhead to a streamer and let some guy photograph me netting it from the creek. When you can act like that and find it funny, you don't need home waters.

What made me need it again was a full, coked-up year of helping to turn my first novel into cinematic junk. That was six years ago, five years after I moved to New Hampshire to write the novel. Since then there has been more going to the mat with Hollywood, publishers, appetites, mortgages, critics, and always, of course, with words. I'm almost forty. I use a compass now some of the time, and I would no more net a dead trout out of home water for a photographer than I would sell my bird dog and move to Beverly Hills.

I have two sons, one seventeen and one twelve. Neither of them has ever shot out a street lamp or run naked down a highway, and I never wrestle with them except for fun. The older one doesn't really like to fish, but the younger one does—loves it, in fact, and in the same indiscriminate, dreaming way that both my father and I did when we were his age. This kid is called Judge.

When I got home to New Hampshire from the movie debacle, skinny and psychologically banged-up, I fished nearly every afternoon of that July and most days I took Judge along. My home water then was a majestic three-mile stretch of the Contoocook River. Judge and I would put in the canoe around four in the afternoon and float until nearly dark. He hadn't learned to use a fly rod yet, so he would throw a spinner while I popped the banks and the rocks like a thirsty man drinking water. We caught a lot of smallmouths that month, and while we caught them—since no recovery process or effort at orientation or pact to get along held him to that spot and moment—Judge would dream out loud about the sea-run brown trout and the bluefin tuna we would catch the following month when we went to Prince Edward Island. Those days in July that year were for me unspeakably sweet and restorative, complete in themselves without needed or wanted reference to any other thing. To Judge, six, with no need for any of the peculiar graces home water bestows, they were, well . . . the Contoocook River.

And so was our stretch of the Blackwater River—with its overgrown banks and still pools, its smart smallmouths and brown trout—only the Blackwater to Judge when it was home water. We'd float it and he'd make me tell him about fishing for black marlin in Australia, even when he'd cast a hair-mouse fly behind a drowned birch tree and watch the eddy come apart as a smallmouth took it.

Catching big wild brook trout in western Maine, sailfish off Stuart, Florida, and bluefish after bluefish over nineteen pounds off the Isles of Shoals had Judge, by this summer, almost permanently blasé about home water. The impression you kept getting was something like, "Well sure I want to fish, but couldn't we at least go over to *Vermont* to do it?"

Then, in August, a movie producer friend of ours came from California to New Hampshire for a four-day visit and brought his new wife and his teenage son and daughter. The boy was a little older than Judge and a lot higher geared. He was dark, good-looking and amusing; he could tell a Ferrari from a Maserati and he knew Jack Nicholson. He also liked to fish. He had fished quite a bit in California and Florida with his father, but he had never caught a good bass, so Judge and I took him one afternoon to our home water.

That water is a lake, one of the most beautiful I've ever seen, three miles from our house and virtually unfished except by my family. There are pickerel in this lake, bluegill, perch, and a lot of big bass, both largemouth and smallmouth. Judge and I have both caught four- to five-pound bass there, and he lost a largemouth this spring that would have gone over six. We fished for these bass with popping bugs, in the evening usually, and we always released them.

Well, we got to this lake—the producer's son, Judge, and I—around five o'clock, an hour and a half before the good topwater fishing starts. Both Judge and I would rather catch one fish on top than five down deep, but the producer's son was after a big bass. So after throwing a floating Rapala for a while with my spinning rod and noting that none of us were getting hits from good fish, he asked if he could put on a plastic worm.

I said sure.

"If you just wait," Judge told him, "until the water cools off, they'll start hitting that Rapala." Since he was sitting in the middle of the canoe, Judge was fishing with a spinning rod, too, using a frog popping plug.

The producer's son put on the worm and caught a couple of pound-and-a-half bass. He was thrilled with the fish, and I told him they were beauties. Judge just looked at them and kept throwing his frog. He shook his head when the producer's son said he wanted to keep the second bass. I told the kid we didn't usually keep the fish out of this lake. He looked disappointed and said he wanted to eat it, so I killed the bass for him.

Waters Swift and Still

Around six-thirty the sun went off the good bank, the breeze lay down, and the lake went totally still. Martins started to skim for insects. A pair of wood ducks flew over whistling, and fish began to dimple the surface. A big pickerel crashed my popping bug, throwing up spray. I hit the fish and pulled back an empty leader.

"*Jesus!*" said the producer's son, looking at the place where the fish hit. "He was so big he broke off your fly."

"Snake," said Judge with disdain. "That was just a snake. He bit it off." Five minutes later he threw his frog up by a rock ten feet from shore and twitched it once. A three-pound largemouth hopped all over it. Judge smiled while he fought the fish, and when he released it he said, "Now *that's* a bass."

The producer's son watched the whole thing, from the splashy hit through the release, without saying anything. Then he took a few more casts with the worm, and asked Judge if he could try the frog.

"You're probably right," Judge told him. "You'll catch more fish with that worm."

We drove home in the dark and the producer's son asked if we could come back and fish the lake early the next morning. I told him I couldn't. There was a silence in the car. "You and Judge could fish though," I said. More silence. "When you get home, make some sandwiches. I'll bring you guys out at five and you can fish until nine or so."

The next morning was foggy and still. I got the boys up at four-thirty and we left the house at five. Both boys were sleepy and grouchy and unhappy with the fog. When we got to the lake I took the canoe off the Jeep and helped them load it. I asked Judge what he wanted for tackle. "I guess we'll just take the spinning rods," he said. His eyes were still half closed and he sounded bored. As I watched them carry the canoe down through the fog to the water, I thought it was likely to be a long morning for them out there. I even hoped that it would be.

I came back at nine-thirty and walked down to the lake. The canoe was just off the point of one of the three islands, a hundred yards off shore. The producer's son was in the bow, casting to the point. Judge was in the stern, his paddle in his lap, and I could hear his voice. The lake was still perfectly calm. The fog had thinned a little without lifting; it rose behind the canoe like a gray-white curtain. The islands, the canoe, the boys, and a dull silver patch of water between us was all there was to see.

I heard Judge laugh. Watching him in the stern, isolated on the water against the curtain of fog, I felt a quick surge of love for him rise and catch in my throat along with something I wanted to say so badly I almost shouted it out across the water. As it happened, I didn't even speak it, then or later—because I didn't have to, and because I had learned on other lakes a long time before that the best lessons have little or nothing to do with words—but if I had, it would have gone like this: *This isn't just a place to wet a line, Judge. This is* home base—*where you start and what you come back to; the place that gives meaning and relevance to every other place you'll ever go.*

"How're you doing?" I yelled.

They looked up and paddled in, taking their time. When they got close I could see they were doing fine. I beached the canoe and the producer's son got out.

"Good morning?" I asked him.

"It was a *great* morning, wasn't it Judge?"

Judge grinned at me. "Jonathan caught some beauties on the frog."

"Keep any?"

"Nope. We released them," said Jonathan.

"How'd you do?" I asked Judge.

"Oh, not so good." He stood up and stretched, and gazed out over the water, looking proprietary and happy. "I fished the worm for a while . . . then I just had a good time watching Jon catch fish."

Fly-Fishing: An Angler's Perspective

Lee Wulff

Fly-Fishing: An Angler's Perspective

IN THE LATE 1400s, Dame Juliana Berners wrote, "Now you must know that there are twelve kinds of impediments which cause a man to catch no fish, apart from other common causes that may happen by chance. The first is if your tackle is not adequate or suitably made. The second is if your baits are not good or fine. The third is if you do not angle in biting time. The fourth is if the fish are frightened by the sight of a man. The fifth, if the water is very thick, white or red from any flood that has recently fallen. The sixth, if the fish do not stir because of the cold. The seventh, if the water is hot. The eighth, if it rains. The ninth, if it hails or snow falls. The tenth is if there is a tempest. The eleventh is if there is a great wind. The twelfth, if the wind is in the east, and that is worst, for generally, both winter and summer, the fish will not bite then. The west and north winds are good, but the south is best."

Then she added, "The trout, because he is a right dainty fish and also a fervent biter, we shall speak next of him. He is in season from March to Michaelmas. He is in clean gravel bottom and in a stream. You can angle for him at all times with a lying or running line except in leaping time and then with an artificial fly."

Dame Juliana's judgments about fishing, set forth in *A Treatise on Fishing with an Angle*, still hold pretty true today. But the tackle and techniques of her time have seen many changes. At the time of her writing, fly-fishing lines were made of horsehair (nine hairs for ordinary trout, twelve hairs for big ones), and rods were of solid wood (of the same types used by bowmen of the day). Reels for holding line and playing fish came later.

The advent of the fishing reel must have constituted the first great change in angling tackle since Dame Juliana's time, because such reels allowed fish to run when fully strong and then be worked back when weakened, meaning that lighter rods and finer lines could be used to capture a fish of a given size and strength. And other improvements and refinements emerged at a steady pace. One of the earliest such changes was the replacement of horsehair with silk for fly lines. Silk was finer, it offered the same strength as horsehair, and it could be oiled for easier handling. In the late 1800s, split bamboo was employed for rods, with the result being rods that were stronger and lighter than the solid-wood ones. Working selectively among the various types of bamboo, rod makers discovered that Tonkin cane had the quickest response and greatest strength-for-weight ratio of any, and Tonkin cane became synonymous, as it is today, with fine bamboo fly rods.

Most of the great changes in fly-fishing tackle and techniques have occurred within my lifetime. In the 1920s, fast-action rods and forward-taper lines were developed, which allowed greater casting distances. Nylon monofilament supplanted drawn silkworm gut to make leaders that were more flexible and easier to use. And rods made from steel and beryllium copper were tested, although split bamboo was and still is popular. The advent in the 1940s of fiberglass rods, fitted with corrosion-proof guides, ferrules, and reel seats, allowed longer and harder fishing on salt water without fear of causing damage to the rod, and made fly rods durable and almost indestructible under normal fishing use.

In the 1950s, plastic fly lines replaced silk, and uniformity of tapers offered even greater casting capabilities. Plastic lines also offered variable densities for floating or sinking, and when forward sections were spliced to slick monofilament shooting lines, casting distances shot out beyond the dreams of old-time anglers.

However crude and cumbersome the tackle of old may seem to us today, it has always had a great charm, a special quality that holds fly fishermen in a common bond. But today's tackle, more so than ever before, has made fishing with a fly rod far more pleasant and effective. The lighter, faster-action rods give needed distance with much less effort, and their uniformly high quality and delicacy allow anglers of today to choose the proper weight and taper of line and length and strength of rod to suit the conditions they fish under. We have taken away the discomforts that used to deter all but the most dedicated. As a result, fly-fishing attracts more and more people every year. Perhaps we are even reaching the point in fly-fishing that was reached in skiing when stretch pants and lighter skis, poles, and boots, and attractive parkas made the ladies more comfortable and better looking on the slopes. Lightweight waders, attractive fishing vests, and lighter equipment, from the rod to the segmented wading staff, have all joined to encourage feminine participation in fly-fishing.

While these changes have opened up the fly fisherman's world to gamefish in all the world's waters, he continues to search for lighter and finer tackle to make his sport even more challenging and pleasurable. But fly-fishing, if it continues as it has for centuries, will never be easy.

One skill that fly fishermen will always have to work on to perfect is fly-casting. It will always call for great coordination of movements over mere seconds of time, and it will always demand rhythm and strength and sensitive control on the part of the angler. Casting will always measure a fly fisherman's skill. And a perfect cast will always give a fly fisherman a heart-warming satisfaction.

Techniques in fishing with the fly rod have changed as much as the tackle. It is amazing to the modern angler that for five hundred years fly fishermen fished for trout and other gamefish using flies with wings that imitated flying insects and that were dragged underwater in a manner no winged insect ever travels. It is almost as amazing to realize how successful fishermen were with such improbable imitations. So many fish were caught with those ridiculous wet flies that it was not until about one hundred years ago, when English angler G. E. M. Skues came along, that more than just a few fly fishermen recognized the simple truth that trout feed mostly on underwater insects (nymphs) that have no wings. And it is fishing nymph imitations that has been central in the development of modern fly-fishing techniques.

Of the American fly fishermen that recognized the importance of nymphs, E. R. Hewitt was among the earliest. A dedicated fly fisherman who was always looking for better ways to catch trout, Hewitt invented many effective fly patterns. Several of his successful nymph patterns were made with Plastic Wood, which he squeezed on a thread-wrapped hook to make a flat nymph body, and black paint that he applied to the back of the body. With these materials, Hewitt was able to create nymph imitations that were far more typical of the naturals found in streams than were the standard wet flies.

Still fresh in my mind are the stonefly nymphs I made in the late 1920s by cutting and sewing pieces of chamois skin onto hooks. But at that time nymph fishing on eastern streams, although practiced by a few and written about to some extent, was still a difficult technique when compared to the standard wet-fly swing. Except to a few of its more efficient practitioners, it was not overwhelmingly effective or accepted. It is important to remember that back then most eastern fly fishermen, who were more advanced in fishing technique than western anglers because of the hard-fished eastern waters they worked, were preoccupied with dry flies and streamers—this latter category of fly gaining popularity in a rush in the mid-1930s when John Alden Knight wrote about the Mickey Finn streamer.

At present, however, the technique of free-drifting nymphs has come into its own. Wide acceptance of it has come as a result of western fly fishermen who had to improve the eastern techniques in order to catch fish that lived on the bottoms of their faster and deeper streams and rivers.

I can remember some years ago looking at the Roaring Fork in Colorado and thinking how difficult it was going to be to fish with the accepted methods of that day. Because the trout were under the turbulent water and feeding near the bottom, fishing to them with the standard wet or dry fly, which only traveled on or near the surface, would not be effective at all. But with the weighted-nymph or nymph-behind-lead technique that the western anglers developed and practiced, these fish can now be reached and caught. And while it will always require considerable skill to drift a nymph well and to sense subtle strikes, it is this deep-drifting technique that overall remains the deadliest method for taking fish with a nymph.

Another aspect to successful nymph fishing came with the development of graphite fibers for rods. While trout can be approached easily in turbulent water and drifts of the nymph need not be made at great distances, holding the heavy bamboo or fiberglass fly rod out at arm's length to achieve short-line, dragless drifts called for strength and endurance. But when the lighter, more sensitive graphite rods came on the market, fishing in the tumbling waters of the West became less exhausting, and eastern anglers who had to make longer casts found they could cast greater distances without feeling fatigued in short periods of time.

Along with the introduction of new techniques, the interest in nymphs has helped to bring us dozens of books on the various kinds of stream insects. Today's fly fisherman knows far more about stream ecology and entomology than the anglers of old ever dreamed of knowing. The wild trout he fishes for, or those that have been stocked but have become accustomed to stream life, have often been caught and released several times, making them wiser and warier. And while they may be more tolerant of the angler's presence in the stream, they now often scrutinize his leader with a practiced eye, and then seeing the bend of a hook hanging down from an otherwise good imitation, at the last moment may turn away, having detected it as a fraud. As tackle and techniques have improved, so have the instincts of our quarry.

Along with developments in tackle and techniques, modern fly-fishing has seen the sport expanded beyond trout fishing. While American fly fishermen trace the origin of their sport and its history to Europe, there is one aspect of fly-fishing that is entirely American. It is the bass fly. Black bass are an American fish and the bass fly is an American development. The first ones were simply overgrown trout flies, some following the more gaudy wet-fly patterns, such as the Parmachene Belle, Yellow Sally, and McGinty, while others, such as the Colonel Fuller, broke away from the trout flies. These big flies led to the first bass bugs and poppers, which were made of cork and feathers or of deerhair, as with Tuttle's Devil Bug, to imitate a heavy bug or mouse.

Bass fishing also expanded the fly-fishing concept, and soon fly fishermen were enjoying the thrill of having a big bass strike a floating bug on a quiet and still evening. The concept of fly-fishing for gamefish other than trout continued to grow, and in no time at all fly-fishing spread to salt water.

Fly-fishing went to the salt water in the 1920s and 1930s. Tarpon were first caught on salmon flies, and these gamefish provided dramatic leaps and superb fishing. Flies for saltwater fish have been made to imitate shrimp and other similar foods, but the mainstay of the saltwater fly rodder is the streamer fly, which imitates a minnow and will catch everything from snook to sharks. Tarpon, snook, and bonefish are the favored fly-rod fish of southern waters, and striped bass and bluefish are the favorites in northern waters. From these species, fly-rodding has spread to all the gamefish of the sea.

Something else was discovered by anglers who took their sport to the sea. What they found was not unlike what they had known while fishing streams, rivers, ponds, and lakes for freshwater fish. They found a beauty on the ocean that is as personal and peaceful as any sunrise or sunset on a sylvan mountain lake. It is a beauty that is found where salt water pushes into the mangroves of Florida or into the rocky coves of New England. There is a magnificence when clouds build up over a shadowy shoreline. Beauty, as well as fishing, was everywhere for the fly fisherman.

This saltwater beauty may be most impressive when the angler is in a small skiff far off the shoreline, surrounded by an endless vista of sea and sky. He may see whales many times the length of his skiff, or great schools of dolphins and porpoises—and perhaps without warning he will be aware of a large fin or a dark-blue shape of a great fish that has come up from the inscrutable depths.

Fly-Fishing: An Angler's Perspective

The sea can also be a lonely place, where solace comes from radio communication, and companionship gives a warm feeling of safety. Any thoughts of gurgling brooks or shaded mountain pools are distant. The sea and its open vistas are a long way from where fly-fishing began. It is a place of adventure, a place of dreams, a place where new ground is being broken and the sense of achievement is as fresh as the air. And it is waiting, all the time, for new challengers.

Saltwater fly-fishing is relatively new, and it is a bit record happy. Because we are still finding places that have bigger fish of a given species than we have caught before, there exists a worldwide race to catch that biggest fish first. To increase the record aspect of saltwater fly-fishing, the lightness of tackle used to catch a fish is classified as well as the size of the fish. While the biggest fish may well have been caught as a result of the angler being lucky, the element of luck is greatly diminished when any angler catches an average-size fish with lighter tackle than has ever been used for that size fish before.

In a lifetime of fishing I can think of no other fish that demanded more of me in the playing than my record one-hundred-forty-eight-pound striped marlin. I caught it on a fiberglass fly rod, which weighed under five ounces and had a single grip, a standard fly line, a reel with a click but without a drag, and a leader with a section of twelve-pound-test monofilament. I was in a fifteen-foot skiff, twenty miles off the coast of Ecuador, and it took four and a half hours to bring the marlin to gaff.

Such big fish are difficult to handle, especially if single-handed fly rods are used, which means the pressure has to come through the angler's arm alone, rather than through the abdomen as it can when a detachable or built-in butt section to the grip is used. In spite of these difficulties, bigger and bigger fish will be caught on fly-fishing tackle, and in the end I think all the species of gamefish will fall to the fly.

The future will see further changes in the equipment fly fishermen use. New materials for lighter and stronger rods will be discovered, as will better materials for fly-tying, and these will make fly patterns even more lifelike. And while fly reels will probably see only minimal changes, fly lines will see a great change.

We will have a change from today's fly-line-and-leader combination, which is simply the joining of a suitable fly-casting line to a section of finer line (called a leader) that is less suitable for casting but far less visible to fish. Fly fishermen who have thought about the true relationship between line and leader know what the future will bring. If six feet of leader will fool fish better than three feet will, why not have the entire line made from leader material? The answer is already on the drawing board. Such a fly line is not that far away.

I have fished with an experimental version of such a line. It was made in Germany from Bonnyl monofilament, and it tapered from four-pound-test at the point to .060 inches in the belly, then back to slightly more than .030 inches for the shooting line. It was great on a warm day, cast beautifully, sliding through the guides effortlessly. When conditions were right, I caught more fish than my comrades. But when the line came off the reel it liked to stay in small coils. And on a cold day I found it impossible to stretch the line so it would straighten out and cast well. Someday, however, a leader material with the characteristics needed for a good fly line will be discovered and today's lines and leaders will be obsolete. Also, as a result of such a line, knots, except for one or two at the tippet, will be eliminated.

Fly-fishing has a promising future, and one that is encouraging in terms of the enjoyment we can expect to derive from it. While tackle will change, and consequently some techniques, a further dimension to the sport—that of conservation—will be an important part of the future of fly-fishing. As we stand on the threshold of the 1980s, fly-fishing is on the verge of a great expansion. We are increasing the productivity and accessibility of our available waters to accommodate the ever-growing number of anglers. I believe we will expand our numbers quickly to the limits our waters will allow, so that the best waters will be designated for no-kill fishing and the marginal waters for stock-and-take-out fishing. And spreading out from the trout streams, we will start bringing back the numbers of other fly-rod species we are presently depleting and protect them for fly-fishing. While changes and developments in the past in the sport of fly-fishing have centered mainly on tackle and technique, in the future the greatest changes that will affect our sport are in regulations and conservation.

I can remember growing up in Alaska when there were no rules about taking fish at all. Then there was only the challenge of taking fish in as many ways as possible. And as one method was mastered, another was practiced. I speared, gaffed, snagged, and snared trout and salmon. And, of all the methods, I enjoyed spearing the most—if it were still legal I'd still be doing it today. The challenge of having to spot the fish in the water, to judge the effect of refraction, to estimate the speed of the current, and to allow the right lead to make up for the fish's speed takes more skill than do a lot of angling methods. Spearing was a great and difficult sport, but once it was mastered it became one of the deadliest. A highly skilled spearsman could practically empty a stream, and as a result spearing was banned. It became acutely apparent that if we wanted to keep fish in our hard-fished waters, we would have to regulate angling methods and eliminate those that were too effective. Double the number of fishermen and the average catch must be halved in order to maintain the same take from the stream.

Fly-fishing, because it is practiced mostly on streams, was the first to suffer from depletion of stocks, and it was also the first to run headlong into the need for conservation measures if it were to survive. But fly-fishing, due to the character of person it involves, was also the first to solve the problem.

The fish in the streams had nowhere to hide. Unlike fish in most lakes, which can choose their depth and roam for miles, fish in streams can seek safety only in pools or under banks. If a stream were only six feet deep at the deepest, then anglers would day after day and week after week put flies and lures and baits within six feet of every fish in the stream. The angling pressure would be so great that the fish could not survive and the stream would be depleted. Where this has happened, attempts to replace the wild stocks with hatchery fish have failed because the hatchery fish had been raised on unnatural foods and could only survive under controlled conditions. As a result, stream fishing slid downhill faster than any other form of fishing.

Presently, catch-and-release, or no-kill, programs are proving to be a major part of the answer to proper management of our streams. And with added regulations, such as single-hook artificial flies only and fly-fishing-only, the future of stream fishing promises to be an enjoyable one.

Through the efforts of organized fly fishermen, no-kill stretches exist on some of our best trout waters. The concept is spreading out to other waters as well. From New York State's Beaverkill and a few rivers in Yellowstone Park, where the no-kill concept began, the catch-and-release programs have spread throughout the country. In California, a law has recently been passed that creates twenty-five miles of no-kill water every year for a long time into the future.

Where one or two fishermen could once work a pool and find only a few fish to rise to their flies, the same pool, as a result of no-kill, now may offer hundreds of fish. And because the fish have been caught and released many times, they have become smarter. Now they offer a great challenge as the angler tries for hours—often in vain—to match the insect they are feeding on. The success of these catch-and-release waters is revealed by the fact that they are crowded with happy anglers while similar waters under normal management are almost barren of fishermen. Stocking for the creel will go on, of course, and grow more sophisticated in the marginal waters, but the best of the trout waters will produce the most, the wildest, and the wiliest trout under the no-kill concept.

Normally, a few fishermen catch the bulk of the fish. Regulations will control this in order to spread the opportunities of the sport more evenly. An example of such a management approach at this writing is the plan to limit the season's catch of Atlantic salmon in some Canadian provinces. A license in New Brunswick next year, for example, may give the holder only twenty tags and require that every salmon in possession must bear a tag. Those who have consistently taken far more than that number will be unhappy. Those who are less skillful, or who may only have a week of the season to fish, will be happy to have those extra salmon, which the more successful fishermen could not take out, still in the streams.

These salmon fishermen, though limited in their take for the season, will not be limited in their angling. According to the plan, an angler may catch and release his two-fish limit every day without having to tag them. The take is limited while the pleasure of angling is not. This management approach reflects the judgment that the value of catching a good gamefish now outweighs its value as food.

Where no-kill regulations seem too drastic but where strict management laws are necessary, there are still other ways to regulate the catches. Restricting the take to fly-fishing-only or to single-hook artificial lures will easily limit catches by demanding greater skill on the part of the anglers who want to take fish out of the stream.

Let me quote another passage from Dame Juliana that is still applicable to modern angling: "For all kinds of fish that feed at the bottom, you must angle for them at the bottom, so that your hooks will run or lie on the bottom. And for all other fish that feed above, you must angle for them in the middle of the water, either somewhat beneath or somewhat above. For always the greater the fish, the nearer he will lie to the bottom of the water; and ever the smaller the fish, the more he will swim above."

Giving the fish the sanctuary of the deep water is another way to limit catches. A fly fisherman has difficulty getting his fly down to the deeper water where the trout spend most of their time. Spinning tackle, however, can cast a lure great distances and put it at the fish's level practically anywhere in the stream. Spinning has been considered too deadly and has been banned on many trout streams. It is completely banned on Canadian Atlantic-salmon rivers. However, surface fishing with wet flies, dry flies, and nymphs means the angler must be skilled enough to make the trout leave his lie to take the fly. Not allowing the fly angler to use lead weights or sinking lines gives the trout the sanctuary of the deep water, and perhaps this is a direction that trout-stream management will take.

If so, in the future, fly-fishing is likely to become divided into three categories: surface, intermediate, and deep. Surface fishing would prohibit the use of any weight of any kind in the fly or on the line, allowing only floating lines. Intermediate fishing would allow weighted flies or small leader weights and slow-sinking lines. Deep fishing would have no restrictions on the weights of flies, sinkers, or the sinking rate of the fly line.

Obviously, casting very light flies is far more pleasant than casting with weight, but it is also less effective. For example, I've already pointed out how effective the technique of nymph fishing is when the angler uses lead weights and weighted flies. But if more people can get more pleasure from surface fishing before stocks of a given water are depleted during the course of a fishing season, it seems more logical to consider applying such a restriction to our fishing than, for example, to shorten the fishing season. On streams where we do not go to no-kill in our management policies, I believe we may find these kinds of restrictions, especially on the small or medium-size streams.

The sport of fly-fishing has a rich history, an exciting present, and an encouraging future. To me, at least, it's a sport that has captured my imagination for nearly a lifetime.

Stillwaters Run Deep

John Merwin

Stillwaters Run Deep

MY POND makes no sense. The questions it posed last summer and fall bite me deeply this winter, and I am impatient for spring and for answers. At times it was generous: fat, wild brown trout that rose freely to almost any fly. At other times it was enigmatic: those days when I neither saw nor raised a fish. But because its occasional rewards are so great, its puzzle continues to pull me. The volumes of stream-trout theory are many, but the obvious lack of information on stillwater trout makes speculation exciting. The Beaverkill and Madison have no mysteries on so grand a scale.

The essentials of our fly-fishing techniques for trout in general are based on the physical fact of current in a stream or river. The current is the most important factor governing the behavior and location of trout in a stream, and as such has become the most important factor in our presentation of a fly. We have grown up learning a river's currents to learn our fly-fishing. Techniques are established. They are comfortable. But in my pond there is neither current nor convention.

And so it is discomforting. Long-familiar trout-stream insects are absent; new forms and species—many unique to stillwaters—must be learned. Names, habitat, behavior, hatching times . . . all new. The fish must be found—not in eddies and swift-water pockets, but over weed beds, in submerged channels, and along ledges often invisible below the pond's unspeaking surface. A rise. A fish. We've found one, finally, and then more rises. But is it one fish just cruising and rising three times in a row, or is it three separate fish, each rising once? The simple task of a river angler casting to a rising fish becomes a fun-house game here in the pond. Now you see it, now you don't. A hall of mirrors.

There is a little pond down the road—quiet and with summer houses all around it—that holds a few small brown trout, which I've caught, and a few very big ones, which I haven't. I fish it often in early spring, because like many small ponds, its fish become active earlier in the season than do trout in the snowmelt-swollen river. I am pushed to this pond then because I can no more bear to fish the freezing river than I can bear not to fish at all.

There is an occasional rise on the calm surface along the opposite shore. The April air feels good. I am ready. The canoe drifts near the point of a rise. I wait, but there is nothing more. Once in a while a small insect pops off the surface and flies away with the characteristically steady flight that distinguishes a mayfly from the more erratically flying caddis. A small mayfly nymph is the logical choice, and another break in the surface down the shoreline gives me a target on which to test the theory. There is a lot of fruitless casting during which there are no more rises.

My best fishing has been in print. That which I've read tells me I'm seeing a cruising trout taking emerging mayflies and that it's a simple matter of intercepting the fish's cruising pattern with the appropriate fly. But these rises are random; there's no perceptible pattern to them. The emergence is very sporadic; it's apparently too sparse a hatch to pull trout to the surface and keep them there. I grow tired of frantically paddling and casting, tired of chasing something I don't really understand. I anchor, chew on a Milky Way, and wish the river were warm enough to fish.

I pull out a fly box, open it, and sit wondering the same thing we all have wondered at such times: what to do when you don't have the least idea what to do. Finally I try a two-fly cast, a pair of Leadwing Coachmen on a longish leader with the same floating line that has so far yielded nothing. The wet flies are old friends; I'll enjoy fishing them if nothing else. I cast and sit. The flies sink, drawing the leader down slowly until the whole affair is held suspended by the buoyant fly line.

The line is pulled down suddenly. I can't believe it—don't believe it—and so don't strike. I twitch the flies carefully back, but nothing happens. Another cast, another slow sinking, the flies again suspended—and another twitch. I'm ready this time. A brown trout—embarrassingly small, but still a trout—flips around next to the canoe. I have discovered the secret. The river is forgotten. I cast again. And again. I think I have learned something, but I don't know what it is.

There is another rise farther down the shore. I paddle over, anchor, cast. The slowly sinking wet flies draw another strike, another midget brown trout. But the game has become to catch a fish, any fish at all. If the wet flies work, a mayfly nymph at the same depth will work better because there are some hatching.

But it doesn't work at all.

The willows have gone from green to gray in the fading light of evening, and it's cold now. There are no more rises. As I paddle back toward the car, I see one of the insects pop off the water and fly toward me. I make a grab from habit and stop to look. It's a damn stonefly! It's small, black, and totally out of place. My stoneflies live in swift riffles; they crawl out onto rocks to hatch. They don't live in ponds. It is unmistakably a stonefly. I'm confounded.

Waters Swift and Still

I have researched, edited, and partly written an anthology on fly-fishing for stillwater trout. In that book, a number of well-known anglers describe various lake-fishing techniques that happen to work at some times in some places. With only a few exceptions, it still strikes me as significant that most of those technical explanations centered on *how* something should be done, rather than *why* it should be done in the first place. It is something like a doctor treating a symptom while having no knowledge of the cause. In medicine, that's no more than a partial answer, and while the stakes are certainly lower, the same reasoning applies to stillwater trout. I am not satisfied with something that only works some of the time. And I now find, having distilled in my own mind the work that went into that book, that several questions keep coming back.

I want to know how to avoid fruitless days in the first place by picking a good trout pond to try among a choice of several. I want to know how the trout in that pond behave and why, and whether or not in a pond with three trout species—brown, brook, and rainbow, for example—if and how each of the three behaves differently. I want to know more about the pond's entomology from an ecological standpoint—that is, not technical nomenclature and generic classifications, but rather behavior, habitat preferences, and relative quantities of various trout-food organisms, insects and otherwise.

This sounds, I admit, like a great deal, but it is no more information than many stream fishermen have had for years and now take for granted. Just because we're fishing in stillwater doesn't mean such information is unattainable, only that it's more difficult to obtain because we can't look it up before a weekend trip.

It becomes all the more frustrating when we do try to look something up, something on lake ecology that might be of value to fishermen, because a large body of technical knowledge has evolved without fishermen. The terms are strange—frightening, perhaps—to a stream fisherman who has never encountered them. And they can be misleading, too.

Biologists and fisheries managers, for example, describe a "good" trout lake as oligotrophic, which I find irritating because our very best trout lakes and ponds are not. Oligotrophic is a term used in lake typology that is generically synonymous with our north country lakes: clear, deep, and cold, with relatively little aquatic vegetation and inhabited, perhaps, by landlocked salmon, brook trout, and smelt. Because their year-round water temperatures remain cold enough for trout, they are habitually classed as trout waters.

Those lakes usually classed as being suitable for bass and other warmwater fishes are called eutrophic. These lakes are generally warmer and support much greater quantities of aquatic vegetation. The life forms in such lakes are typically more abundant in terms of individuals and variety of species than they are in oligotrophic lakes. Although eutrophic lakes are more productive, they are often too warm for trout.

From a fly fisherman's point of view, oligotrophic lakes—the "good" trout lakes—are often difficult to fish. Relatively low fertility and steeply sloping shorelines often mean that insect populations will be sparse. The ideal, perhaps, is a lake or pond that is eutrophic in every sense except water temperature—a fertile lake with abundant vegetation and water temperatures that remain low enough all year to support trout.

Some of these lakes are legend: Henrys Lake in Idaho is one such. It has abundant vegetation, cold water, a wide variety of organisms on which trout feed, and a substantial population of good trout that come well to flies. And while there are numerous small ponds in the Rockies and throughout the West that are generally comparable to Henrys Lake, there are fewer in the Midwest and Northeast.

But whether it is in the West, the Midwest, or the East, consistency, in my mind, is a primary criterion for any good trout lake or pond. Some stillwaters, however, while not consistent enough for year-round flyfishing, have a special hatch or other event that makes them worthwhile. There is, for example, a fine hatch of the giant *Hexagenia* mayflies that takes place on many trout lakes from northern Connecticut north to Canada for a few days each June or July. There is one such hatch on Lake Memphremagog, which straddles the border between Vermont and Québec, and about which a friend of mine who lives on the lake has told me often. That lake has a substantial population of rainbows over five pounds that surface-feed on that twilight hatch. But the hatch lasts only a few days, and my timing must be exact. So far, it has not been. For the rest of the year, the rainbows in the lake belong to the people who spend more time fighting trolling rigs than fish.

I once lived next to a small northern trout stream and spent an hour or two every day all season for several years fishing the short stretch nearest the house. It held all wild fish, a mixture of browns, brooks, and rainbows. After a while I started to realize that there were significant differences in behavior among the three species in the same stretch of water, even in the same pool. Things finally reached a point at which I'd look at a pool and then determine which of the three species I'd catch by deciding where to cast. It eventually became a game I played with myself, like calling balls and pockets in a pool game. Brown in the prime feeding lie. Rainbow in the riffle. Brookie back in the slough. Eventually we moved away, and the game was something I forgot until I started fishing trout ponds.

During one recent season, I happened to concentrate on a pond that held, among other fish, both brown and rainbow trout. The pond had occasionally heavy caddis hatches, a very few mayflies, good midge hatches, and heavy flights of ants in early fall. There was, in other words, plenty of surface food to which both kinds of trout often rose. It wasn't until the end of that season that I began to notice a dramatic difference in the way the two kinds of trout were surface-feeding. I often encountered the rainbows—both singly and in small groups—as they strung their riseforms together across the entire width of the pond. At other times, and depending on what was hatching, a pod of them might concentrate their feeding in a single area of the small lake. Rarely were they in the same place either all day or on two consecutive days. That was really what I expected to find. Rainbows, after all, are wanderers, and surface-feeding trout in a lake are *supposed* to be cruising.

But there were other rises, too, in a little shoreline cove, off a certain hemlock, near a particular rock, and in other places. Evening after evening until ice locked the lake away, the same fish appeared to be rising in the same places, much like the favored feeding lies of trout in a stream. When I caught these fish, they were invariably brown trout. They were feeding in well-defined beats, rarely overlapping, each beat covering an area of the pond no more than twenty yards square. Yes, I have seen browns cruising, and yes, I also realize they'll follow schools of forage fish (especially in large reservoirs and big lakes). But in this and in other small ponds I have raised a brown trout in a particular spot—defined within a range of a few feet—and then done so again both the next day and the next week. Always a brown, never a rainbow. That is central in my fishing thoughts now, and the problem compounds itself.

There is a pond in the middle of our village that holds both native brookies and an occasional rainbow. The water is quite clear, and I sometimes bring my small children there to watch the trout swimming around. I finally noticed that while the rainbows never seemed to stop cruising—even without a hatch—the brook trout cruised only when actively feeding, which was seldom. Most of the time the individual brook trout suspended themselves just off the bottom, motionless, in the shade of a bankside bush or overhanging grass. If I flipped a twig on the water nearby, they would swim over, investigate, then swim back to the same place and rest once again. If we were careful, we could do this without spooking them, and last year we had fun making a game out of it.

But it was also puzzling. Do all brookies in lakes act this way? Do the brown trout in the pond I often fish do this? I haven't seen them do it, but sometimes, when they appear from nowhere to take a fly, it seems as if it might have been this sort of thing—an attack from ambush. Suddenly it seems to me that fly-fishing for stillwater trout, so long regarded as a random pursuit, is not the least bit random. The possibility is exciting.

In the last few years, much research has gone into the spatial requirements of trout, especially brown trout, in streams. Individual fish have been reported to have something analogous to "character." Anglers seem to have known this for some time while scientists are just now discovering it. Territoriality of a sort has been demonstrated in some trout populations. But these observations have all been made with regard to trout in streams, where the current exerts an influence on the distribution of trout. Does a similar sort of reasoning apply to stillwater trout, trout living where there is no current? It is easy to understand why a trout holds behind a boulder in a rapid stream. That makes not knowing my pond more difficult to bear.

I remain uncomfortable with trout lakes and ponds. On a trip to a new area, I would still probably try any available stream before trying a pond. I am used to learning streams and can often do so quickly. I am still unaccustomed to learning ponds, but I have learned enough to no longer avoid them, as many people do, solely for that reason.

The last day of the season is a special day, the fishing closest to the midwinter recollections that follow. Trout ponds have been more in my fishing for the last couple of years, and have become my last day's fishing as well.

Our Vermont season ends in late October. It has snowed three weeks before, but the ground is again bare and brown. The first flush of grouse season is a month old, the mad invasion of deer hunters only two weeks off. The ski boom hasn't started. Things are quiet, and on this day my pond is quiet, too.

A cold, misting rain doesn't blow but rather sits on the pond below the mountain. The air and water temperatures are the same: 50 degrees. My hands are cramped by cold around the paddle shaft as I slide over the water. When the entire world seems to have stopped, the trout are rising

Stillwaters Run Deep

in the pond. Not many rises, but a few gentle swirls. The ever-present hatching midge is pinned to the surface by the cold. Wet wings stay wet. The little insects are unable to fly and unable to get back to the security of the weeds and mud from which they ascended.

My hands are too cold and stiff for fine tippets and small flies. I can't tie the knots. It is the last day, and I must catch a fish, my trout for the winter. I gnaw the leader back and awkwardly tie on a white Muddler. Cast and strip. Cast and strip. Work hard. Try to keep warm. Finally a fish comes from I don't know where. A lovely brown trout, bright and hard and sharp, thumps against the canoe and I release it. And I'm satisfied because I have done what I set out to do. Because I can master my pond. Sometimes.

October:
A Northwest
Idyll

Steve Raymond

October:
A Northwest Idyll

OCTOBER is more than just a month. It is a feeling, a feeling almost strong enough to touch, reaching out to every living thing, giving the signal for change and movement. It hurries the salmon, trout, and steelhead on their way, hurries the angler in pursuit of them, hurries the tattered formations of geese heading south, and hurries the leaves in their dying. It is the culmination of all the other months, the last, best moment of the year.

So very much happens in October. Although its thirty-one days are as many as are allotted any month, they are not time enough. In October, the rainbows in the interior lakes are fat and strong; the last of the bright summer steelhead are returning from the sea; the salmon are rolling restlessly in the estuaries, and the cautious cutthroat prowl the shallow waters of the coast. To go in search of one may mean forfeiting the best chance to catch another, and so October always is a month of difficult decisions for an angler. That is why I have trouble coping with October, even though it is my favorite month and I look forward to its coming and feel regret when it has passed.

Once I tried to squeeze every moment from that magic month, to fish each day from earliest dawn to darkest twilight so there would be no chance of missing any of the opportunities October so generously af-

Waters Swift and Still

fords. But now that I am a little older and, perhaps, a little wiser, that no longer seems a practical approach. Instead, I now try to place myself in harmony with the natural rhythm of the month and fish where and when my senses tell me that I should. It is by no means a perfect formula, but it works well enough, and it is not quite so strenuous as fishing every day from dawn to dusk.

Usually I begin the month on Dry Falls Lake—and only partly for the fishing. October's first weekend is time for the annual outing of fly fishermen from Seattle, and there is always a big campfire, a huge pot of stew, a keg of beer, and a lot of good talk—and those things alone are worth the trip. So is the sight of the aspens that grow along the river bottoms and in the folds of the Cascade's eastern slopes. They are ablaze early in October, their leaves dancing with the colors of hot flame. The color lasts only briefly; the strong west winds that blow through the passes see to that. By month's end there will be only a few leaves left, and the last may fall on the season's first snow, leaving a gold-and-scarlet litter on the gleaming hillsides.

But Dry Falls Lake itself is a spectacular sight, surely one of the grandest scenes on the continent. It lies at the foot of the ancient falls of a once-mighty river, a forebear of the Columbia but much larger than its child. The river had come and gone long before men came to the country, but the dry falls are its monument. The modern lake, formed by seepage, occupies the catch basin formed by the falls. It is surrounded by desert, and it is hard to think of the place as ever having been as wet as it must have been when that awesome, ancient flow of water was plunging over the cliffs. What now is desert must then have been bathed in a great, glistening cloud of spray rising from the falls. Today, it is carpeted with dry bitterbrush and sage and huge basalt boulders left behind by the prehistoric floods.

There are heavy trout in Dry Falls Lake, mostly rainbows with a scattering of browns. They like it in the shallows in October, back where the weeds are thick and cover is easy to find. The season is too late for heavy hatches, and there is only an occasional delinquent mayfly or straggling midge for the trout to rise to. But they rise anyway, leaving delicate dimples on the still surface. No one seems certain why they rise, since the surface is devoid of visible food. But no one complains, either, and the trout can be made to come vigorously to a dry fly if it is twitched a time or two. No dimples then—they hit with a crash, throwing spray.

When a strong trout lunges to a moving fly, the shock is often more than a light leader tippet can stand. But even if the tippet holds, your task has just begun: Dry Falls trout are well trained, and when they feel the hook they dive quickly for the weeds. Often that is the last you will see of them; they literally disappear into a jungle of clinging growth, taking your fly with them. If you are lucky you will get most of your leader back. And if you react quickly enough and put on all the strain the tackle will withstand to keep the fish up, swimming near the surface, you will have a chance to land it.

The rainbows are uniformly fat, with bold red ribbons on their sides. The browns are chunky, too, and cream-colored, with crimson spots along their flanks. They are all strong trout and they do not surrender easily. They test your skill to the limit before they submit to a waiting net. On a good day, you may take several fish over two pounds, perhaps one or two over three. The regulations allow you to keep only one fish, and one is enough when the fish are of such size. The regulations assure there will always be such fish in Dry Falls Lake.

In October the sun's low light causes strange shadows to track across the ramparts of the dry falls. The cattails at the margins of the lake are alive with the sound and movement of yellow-headed and red-winged blackbirds. Comical coots bob and splash in the shallows. Toward evening comes the haunting, honking, long-distance call of geese, sometimes flying so high that you must look long and hard before you see their tiny, dark silhouettes against the deep-blue, autumn sky. The cliffs of the dry falls collect the sound and pass it around the walls of the great stone amphitheater so that it is somehow amplified, and it echoes and re-echoes a long time before dying.

It is a good place to begin this most productive month, to stalk the shallows and make a careful cast toward a dimpling trout, to twitch the fly and watch it disappear in a spectacular, splashing rise, to see an angry trout rip the still surface. Dry Falls never disappoints.

In October's second week I begin to think more of steelhead than of trout. A small stream not far from the city harbors a fine run and the fish are there, it seems, only in October. Common sense says they must be there later in the year as well, but the river is less friendly then, the fishing not so pleasant, the fish not as bright or as easy to find. So October is the time to seek these gleaming, sea-run fish.

Once the river was fished heavily, but in recent years it seems to have been forgotten by most anglers, and that is fine with me. The steelhead run is small and the stream too easily accessible; too much pressure would be fatal to it. And so I go there by myself, almost always to the same productive pool, following a familiar path through the dry woods with crisp, newly fallen leaves crackling underfoot. The pool is in a narrow canyon, bordered by steep, moss-stained, rocky walls with a slim opening at the top where a strip of pale-blue sky shows through. Usually it is still Indian summer in October's second week, with mist in the mornings and still afternoons that carry a hint of woodsmoke in the air. The vine maples are the west-slope counterpart of the aspens, and while not quite as vivid in their rusty hues, they are still bright enough against the cedar, fir, and spruce that cling precariously to the canyon walls. The autumn scents and sights are all familiar. I know this place, I feel good here.

Most especially I know the pool. Although not far from a heavily traveled road, it is well hidden in the canyon. The pool is so deep and quiet that its surface seems almost still, but the current is there, deceptively strong. The pool holds a secret: a great old alder that fell into the river in some season past and was carried by the current to this place. Its tangled roots are wedged among the rubble on the bottom and its thick trunk lies parallel to the flow, with its twisted branches at the upstream end of the pool. The years have coated it with a yellow-brown growth of algae that makes it difficult to see, even when the sun is directly overhead and the water is low. But the steelhead know it is there, and they usually lie in the shelter of the upper branches. Almost always there is at least one fish there, sometimes two or three.

October: A Northwest Idyll

Those branches took many flies from me before I learned exactly how to cast so that the current would carry the fly just past them without hanging up, but close enough so a steelhead could see it. An old snag back in the woods serves as my silent guide: By lining myself up with it and carefully measuring the necessary length of line, it is possible to make the cast.

The fish, if any are there, usually respond to the fly's first or second swing, following it from beneath the log to nail it hard when the line straightens in the current. When the light is just right you can see them, and my fishing diary reminds me of a day when three fish followed the fly as it swung past the log and I wrote that they "looked for all the world like a Tommy Brayshaw painting."

But if the pool is an easy place to hook a fish, it is not an easy place to land one. These are wild fish, always strong, and it is a difficult task to hold them in the pool and fight them there without losing them in the threatening limbs of the drowned alder. But they must be held, for below the pool is a wild stretch of boulder-strewn water flowing through a constricted reach of canyon where it is impossible to follow a running fish. If they get down into that water, as they sometimes do, you have lost them.

There is no finesse to it. You try to make the fish leap instead of run, and if they do run you try to turn them. It is a struggle of brute strength, and sometimes the tackle is not quite equal to the task. If it is not, the leader parts and the fight ends quickly. We are about even, the steelhead and I. I have lost just about as many as I have landed.

The struggle disturbs the pool so badly it must be rested for hours before there is any chance of taking another fish from it. Sometimes I leave it and look upstream at water that is less reliable. Sometimes I just sit and rest, enjoying the quiet, subtle sounds of the pool and the sights around it—the trees on the canyon walls, bright in autumn gold; the gleaming dust of fresh snow sometimes visible along the canyon rim; the little wreaths of mist that float among the tallest firs. And after the pool is rested, I return to it and try again. Even if I should fail to get a second strike, I can leave knowing that the next day chances are good another fish will be waiting. The pool is simply too good a spot for any fish to pass it by without stopping to rest under its sheltering, secret log. It is an exciting place, one of the best things about October, and I could easily spend much more time there. But then I would miss the salmon entering the estuaries.

I don't know how they find their way back; no man knows, really. But they do. From the dark, trackless reaches of the stormy North Pacific they return, following the coast past countless sounds and bays to the mouth of the Strait of Juan de Fuca. There they turn and work their way into the labyrinthine waters of Puget Sound, dividing into separate races and runs, searching out the estuaries of their native rivers. And there they wait, giant chinooks, precocious little jacks, and cohos grown sleek and silver on rich sea feeding. They will wait until the rains swell the rivers and high tides lift them over the shallow flats and gravel bars at the river mouths, and then they will begin their spawning ascent. But while they are still in the estuaries they are vulnerable to a knowing angler with a fly rod.

I know of one short stream that flows down from the hills and into a deep ditch next to a road. It looks like nothing more than a drainage ditch, which in part it is, but from its ignominious roadside reach the stream meanders through a swampy thicket to the edge of a long, shallow, saltwater bay where its tiny flow is lost in the surging tide. But small as it is, the salmon somehow are able to find it, and it hosts a run all out of proportion to its size.

There is no fishing for the salmon once they enter the little stream because they are too visible and vulnerable to offer any sport. But while they are in the estuary they offer an exciting challenge.

The estuary was once a place where log rafts were made up to be towed to distant lumber mills, but now the only evidence of those days are the neat rows of weathered pilings where the sea gulls sit and face the wind. Herons stride the salt flats on ungainly legs at low tide and kingfishers chatter in the limbs that sag along the beach. Grebes bob and feed in the changing currents, and mallards wing past in wary flight. There is plenty to watch if the fishing is poor. But it seldom is.

When the tide is at its height, the waiting salmon grow restless, rolling and plunging and sometimes throwing themselves high out of the water. They do not take a fly well, but they will follow it curiously, often coming right to the edge of the boat before they turn away. And always there are a few that will take—that will seize the fly in a rush and begin a long, sizzling run across the shallow flats. Then they leap, high and twisting—not once but half a dozen times—and whichever way the tide is flowing they will use it to advantage. Their fight is always spectacular, always long, always tough, and very often it ends when the leader catches on the sharp edge of an oyster shell or on toothlike barnacles on the submerged portion of a piling. But sometimes it ends in victory for the angler, with a played-out fish alongside the boat, perhaps a six- or eight-pound coho or a smaller jack chinook. Then the fly is twisted from the tough gristle of the jaw so that the salmon is again free to go about nature's business.

It is exciting, unpredictable fishing, often frustrating when the salmon refuse to take, but wildly rewarding when they do. And sometimes the rewards include a rare sight. I remember one day when the gentle wind died, the clouds parted, and sunlight poured through on flat water long enough to disclose a great school of salmon, hundreds of them, gliding like bright ghosts through the shallows. Only October seems to offer such sights.

The salmon keep their own schedule, and their arrival time is never certain. They will come in October, beyond doubt, but they may be early or they may be late. Some days, when you expect to find them, they are not there. But if that should happen there is still a good chance of salvaging the day, because October is also a time when the cutthroat come into the estuaries. These shy, secretive fish patrol the beaches, close in, feeding on all the tiny, teeming life they find in the gravel and the saltwort and the oyster beds. On a calm day they may reveal their presence with an occasional dimple or a rare splashing rise, and nearly always such a sight means not just one fish but a whole school of them. They take a wet fly and a dry even better, and I have had many fine days casting a small dry fly along the leading edge of the tide, watching cutthroat rise to take it freely.

Waters Swift and Still

One year I was hurt and could not fish—a shoulder injury that meant five months of pain, frustration, weakness, and slow rehabilitation. It was October when I finally felt strong enough to fish again. I chose a good day, a mild, almost springlike day, and drove down narrow roads whose edges were buried under fallen leaves, enjoying the sights and sounds and scents of the outdoors after having missed them for so long. Fading orange and yellow foliage was still clinging to the maples and alders around the bay, and the sky held a thin overcast that occasionally parted to welcome bright sunshine. A gentle southeasterly breeze stirred the surface of the bay lightly, and beyond the western ridge a thick column of smoke rose from burning slash, adding the perfect hint of haze and scent to the bright autumn day.

I began fishing tentatively, unsure of my timing or my strength, but the cutthroat soon began to make me forget my doubts. The fishing was as good as the day itself, some of the best cutthroat fishing I have ever had. And when it was over I had released sixteen cutts and a small jack coho. Although it was October, that day seemed like the beginning of the season to me.

The sea-run cutthroat is a handsome fish, strong and bright in its lime-and-silver dress, and it comes easiest on days of dark overcast or rain. By late October there are usually many such days. The rapid change of the season is well under way by then, the heavy, gray overcast moving in from the ocean to settle down in the valleys. A cold, steady drizzle falls throughout the day, and sometimes in the afternoons the wind begins to come in sullen, violent gusts that strip the last leaves from the trees. Rivers swallow them up and carry them along like a school of small, brightly colored fish on a downstream migration. The migration ends where the leaves collect in the shallows, eddies, behind logs, or on the bottom in the quiet pools.

In late October the rain swells the rivers and draws the fish up into them, and all the waiting is over. Movement is at its peak, the rhythms of the month suddenly accelerate, and the fisherman's opportunities are nearly at an end. But if high water hides the salmon and steelhead, there may be one more chance for rainbows in the lakes, where the trout are still feeding.

October: A Northwest Idyll

On the last morning of one October, a friend and I set out for Merry Lake and found fresh snow falling in the passes that persisted as we drove eastward into the desert of the Columbia Basin. When we arrived at the lake it was shrouded in mist and surrounded by snow. We cracked thin layers of ice around the shore to launch our boats.

The mist froze where it touched the ground, forming a crust over the newly fallen snow. Ice formed in our rod guides, building up with each cast until it was necessary to dip the rods in the lake to thaw it. Ice also formed in tiny gleaming crystals on the line as it was retrieved from the still, dark surface of the lake. Our hands and feet quickly grew numb, and I can remember pressing my fingers into the bowl of my glowing pipe and feeling nothing.

At times the mist was so thick we could not see one another, although we were not fishing far apart, and so we shouted to stay in touch. After two hours we were chilled so thoroughly we went ashore and shook the ice and snow from old, dried sagebrush limbs and started a reluctant, smoldering fire. We stood around it in an effort to warm ourselves, but the fire did nothing to dispel the chill. The cold reached through our clothing, through our flesh, right into the marrow of our bones. It was the cruelest, coldest, October day I've known.

But in the afternoon the temperature rose slightly so there was no longer any ice forming in the guides. The trout grew more active and began to take, and four large rainbows came my way along with half a dozen smaller fish, and I felt amply rewarded despite the hardships of the day. Afterward, in the warm truck on the way to town, the feeling began returning to my hands, and it felt as if a thousand tiny needles were being inserted in them. Still later, after a thick steak and a strong drink or two, the bitter cold had become a distant memory and we thought only of the fine trout we had caught and of how warm and comfortable we were. We had played out October to the very last, and if it had offered us one more day I think I would have stayed at home.

When October is over we look back and wonder how it could have passed so quickly. But one such month is quite enough—if there were others they would only spoil us.

Just a Rod Away

Geoffrey Norman

Just A Rod Away

THE ROD, like everything else packed in the back of my car, was brand new. I had taken it out of the aluminum carrying tube perhaps a dozen times, first to admire it and then to take it down to the park where a friendly young man who belonged to one of the city's casting clubs showed me how to use it properly. But that had been casting to plastic rings anchored in a shallow, lifeless pond. Now, after owning the rod for almost six months, I was going to use it where it was built to be used—on a trout stream.

Now, I was no kid. I was in my late twenties, a veteran, and a rising young magazine editor. I owned my automobile outright, and I played the stock market and bet the NFL football games. Nor was I an absolute novice as an angler, since I had caught fish as exotic as wahoo and northern pike. I was not even an absolute newcomer to fly-fishing. I had caught largemouth bass as large as seven pounds on an old fiberglass rod that disappeared after I went into the service. And a few months earlier I had caught a five-pound smallmouth one memorable morning on a borrowed fly rod up in Canada. A few minutes before I caught the fish, I saw a bald eagle, the first that I had seen wild in twenty years. It was one of those interludes that come to you in fishing and are with you the rest of your life.

Waters Swift and Still

But I had never used a fly rod on a trout stream. There were good reasons for this—some obvious and sound, others not so obvious but, I think, just as sound. Maybe even more so. I had done most of my growing up in the South, the greatest part of it on the Gulf Coast where there were simply no trout to be caught. So I learned to fish for bass. And when I thought I was good enough, I moved up from bait-casting to fly-casting. I got to be pretty good with a frog-pattern popping bug around a lily pad. It was one of the joys of my young life.

In those days, kids read about their enthusiasms. If you were a big sports fans, there were magazines full of articles about favorite athletes, along with full-page color pictures that you could tear out of the magazine and hang on your wall. If you were hot on cars, there were magazines that carried all the latest information on the new models and advertisements for tools and kits to help you rebuild the old ones. And if you cared about hunting and fishing, there were some fine publications full of stories and tips, advertisements to drool over, and even an occasional brush with literature. Nowadays, when specialization is the word, it is hard to remember that *Field & Stream* published *The Old Man and the Boy* by Robert Ruark as a serial. My father and I would try to beat each other to the mailbox to get at the next installment. Writers as fine as Vance Bourjaily and Philip Wylie used to appear regularly in the outdoor magazines.

And I read them avidly, like so many young boys of my generation. After a while I did not pay that much attention to the articles about bass fishing. I was getting to that point where I had heard most of it—and even to the point where I thought I knew more than some of the writers. But I read about trout and salmon eagerly, and I began to think of that as "real fishing." For one thing, the tackle was so fine. Split-cane rods instead of the tough, old fiberglass tool that I had picked up for less than twenty dollars. Trout fishermen still wrote about silk lines and gut leaders. They had formulas for leader tapers—some of their leaders ran fifteen feet—and they carried these lovely willow creels. Bass fishermen used five or six feet of available monofilament line for a leader and put the fish they caught on a metal stringer. They could have been catfish.

Then there were the flies. Wets and drys in all sorts of patterns and sizes. A good trout-fishing writer could give you five different flies in the course of his opening paragraph. By the time you finished the article, you would be exposed to a dozen or more, and the confidence with which he selected his flies, changing them whenever he got a refusal, was impressive. It was too much for a boy who owned perhaps ten cork popping bugs that he divided into two categories—big ones and small ones.

Furthermore, trout fishermen went to the best places. Cold northern streams where there were no other fishermen, not to mention the water skiers, duck hunters, and alligator poachers that bass fishermen often had to put up with. The trout men did some of their fishing in places where English was not spoken. And on this continent, their rivers had names like the Snake and the Rogue.

In ten years of reading those magazines I developed a healthy inferiority complex. I would, I decided, never be a trout fisherman. The game was too refined for the likes of me, who sometimes—the shame of it—would put on a *very* small bug and spend an hour or two catching a stringer of bluegills. I would never understand opera, either, or read Homer in the original Greek; some things were just not in the cards. I suppose I resigned myself to all of this at some time or another. The worst part of it was knowing that I would never feel firsthand what was described in some of my favorite writing. Not to be able to live what Nick Adams lived in "Big Two Hearted River" seemed a real loss.

And probably I never would have fished for trout if it had not been for the rod that lay in the back of the car, now, with all the other brand-new gear, some of it still smelling like the fishing department of Abercrombie's where it all came from, including the rod.

I had bought all of that gear—except the rod. It had been given to me by a man who will always be a friend, and who taught me a lot when I still had so much to learn that I thought I knew it all. He was my boss as well as my friend and he handled both roles superbly. He was a city boy, Jewish and raised in the Bronx. He had a quick mind and was sincerely curious about those things he had not seen up close. So he asked me

Waters Swift and Still

about the South and I tried to tell him about it, just as he tried to tell me about the city. Then he traveled to Alabama with me on two or three occasions and I spent some time with him in New York. It was an odd friendship, but solid and genuine. We liked each other.

We also did favors for each other, and one day he decided that something I had done for him called for some sort of special thanks. It wasn't really that much of a favor, but he had a sense of honor fierce as any Southerner's and he felt obliged to do more than say thanks. Since I had just come back from a trip to Canada and some fine smallmouth fishing and had talked about it until all my friends were bored with it, he decided to get me a fly rod.

So he went to Abercrombie's on his lunch hour one day and asked the clerk for the best rod they carried. Something fine. Being from the Bronx and having never been fishing in his entire life, he wasn't able to answer the clerk's questions. He simply said he wanted the best. Fishing poles were fishing poles. What's to select?

He came into my office after lunch and handed me one of the last Orvis rods built by Wes Jordon, the master builder. It was their basic trout rod, eight feet long, about four ounces, made of split bamboo with the deep finish that is characteristic of Orvis rods, a product of their heat-tempering process. I slipped the rod out of the aluminum tube and then the cloth bag and joined it at the ferrule, which locked up snugger than my old fiberglass stick ever had. Just putting that Orvis together you knew it was fine. I gave it a little action with my wrist and the rod felt strong and responsive. I knew that I had something special in my hand.

So I thanked my friend and he smiled with the satisfaction that comes from giving a gift that hits home. I put the rod up in the corner of my office and looked at it for the rest of the day. That night I took it home to my apartment. And I decided that I would have to learn how to become a trout fisherman even if I was old and unworthy and had been weaned on bass and bluegills. I could not own a rod that fine and not use it . . . and use it well. The physical gift and the human impulse behind the giving of it both demanded nothing less.

Just a Rod Away

It was November, so I had a few months to learn about trout fishing before I could actually go out and do it. Eager as I was to use the rod, I looked on the next few months as something of a grace period, and I started in on my homework.

I started buying books and reading them at night, trying to learn the actual meaning of terms that had always been obscure. Just what in the hell was a 6X tippet? A roll cast? A drag-free float? And so on and so forth. I studied and I learned and I wondered if I could ever put all of it together. I decided to save the entire business of flies for last. I'd never be able to learn all those patterns from books. When the time came, I would buy some flies and learn them as I fished with them.

Now, there are a lot of books published about fly-fishing and a lot of them are very smug, erudite, and daunting to the man who sits in his city apartment reading them and trying to learn the fundamentals. A few of the books I picked up were absolutely infuriating, written by men who seemed more interested in protecting the mysteries than in unraveling them. Their prose was prolix and their tone was condescending and I finally said to hell with them.

I settled on a few congenial souls who seemed to think that fishing was something that one first does for pleasure and never for status. The books of A. J. McClane, Ray Bergman, and Peter Barrett were very helpful. Charles Waterman's *Modern Fresh and Salt Water Fly Fishing* was the closest thing I had that winter to a companion. Chatty, wise, and reassuring. And, praise the Lord, a book that gave bass fishing with the fly rod a place right up there on the front of the bus. After I'd read Waterman's book two or three times I began to feel like I might be able to do right by my new rod after all.

Spring was getting close when I discovered the casting club and the helpful young man who showed me how to smooth out a very rough stroke and make my brand new, peach-colored fly line turn over like it was blown by a soft wind instead of shot from a gun. I began to go to the

Waters Swift and Still

park with my rod at dawn, before there was any traffic or any hecklers, and I would cast for an hour, trying to imagine how it would be on moving water. After I lost my concentration and got lazy, I would break the rod down and put it back in its case, go home to the apartment, and change for work. Every day, I was thinking more and more about Opening Day. Up in Michigan.

I did not know where to go. Just for fun one day I studied a map of Michigan until I found the Two Hearted River. It looked to be seven hundred or eight hundred miles from Chicago and so far north that it might still be covered with ice on Opening Day. I needed something a little closer to home. So I called a poet I knew who lived in Michigan and who loved to fish and asked him where I should go. "Baldwin," he said. "The Pere Marquette River." I went back to the map, found it, and planned my route. This was probably a month before Opening Day.

The next week I went to the catalogs and back to Abercrombie's and bought waders and a vest and a leader wallet and all kinds of fly boxes . . . things that I used once or twice and that have followed me through three moves and have never been used again and never will be. I don't need a leader wallet any more or a device to help me knot my fly on. But this was going to be my first season, with my new rod, and I wanted to be ready.

The season opened on a Saturday in early May. On Friday I left work early and, with my car full of new gear, drove to Baldwin, some two hundred and twenty miles away. It was before the fifty-five speed limit and I made it in less than four hours. There was still a little light when I got to town. I studied the river from the bridge. It looked high and dark, not at all like the trout streams of my reading or my imagination. It didn't even look safe to wade.

I got a cabin on the banks of the river and that night I went through all of my tackle. I sorted a few flies that I had bought from Orvis in one of those basic selections. I studied each fly and tried to learn how to recognize it. I tied up some extra leaders, which more than filled my leader wallet. I must have had thirty leaders. I greased my fly line even though it had not spent a total of five hours on water. I tried to sleep, but did not. Instead, I listened to the river and tried to imagine that I could hear the water level falling.

In the morning I bought a license and some flies. The man who sold me the flies had been fishing the river for more than twenty years. He had moved up from Detroit and he ran a little shop. When I told him how raw I was, he helped me and sold me some flies that he said would work if there were any hatches, which he doubted since the river was so high. I thanked him and said I would be back. I was . . . to the tune of several hundred dollars over the next five years.

I don't have to tell anyone who has ever fly-fished anything more about my day. It was awful. I fell in the river before I'd made twenty casts. I spent hours freeing my fly from the alders that grew along the banks of the river and that I'd never had to take into consideration when I was casting from a platform in a city park. I could not master moving water, locate fish, identify insects, or get warm. When I got back to my little cabin at dark, thinking only of a hot shower and a glass of dark whiskey, I felt like I had let my rod down.

The next day was more of the same, less the dunking. I considered it some sort of victory that I had learned to walk. One of these days, perhaps, I would learn to run. Now, if I could just keep the fly out of the tag alders and get a nice drag-free drift from time to time, maybe I could actually catch a fish, though I had not seen the first rise or, for that matter, the first hatching mayfly. My spirits were as low as the sullen sky that stretched west and north across all the vastness of Lake Michigan.

Then, an hour before I had to leave the water and Baldwin and head back to the city, I caught a fish. I was casting a little Royal Coachman that had gotten soaked and I hadn't bothered to dry and refloat. It did not seem worth the trouble. I was flicking the little fly out ahead of me, downstream, as I made my way back to the car. It had been a sorry baptism for my new rod.

I almost missed the strike. In fact, I would have if I had not been fishing downstream and the line had not been pulled tight. My presentation, such as it was, could not have been further from a drag-free drift. The strike of the fish set the hook, and when I realized what had happened, I played my catch with all the care I could manage. I didn't want to lose this fish, no matter how artlessly he had been hooked.

It was a rainbow, all six inches of him. One thing I had learned studying those books was how to identify the various trout, and this was a rainbow. I admired him as long as I dared then popped the hook loose with my brand-new forceps and let him swim away. I felt much better. In fact, I felt the most comforting of all the emotions—hope. We had to start somewhere, my rod and I, and this was it. With a miserable weekend and one tiny trout, hooked by accident.

I went back to Baldwin almost every weekend of that trout season, and I got an education. Within a couple of months, I was catching small fish fairly regularly. And I was losing less than six flies a day in the tag alders and I never fell down anymore. I could keep forty feet of line out and I could actually make a kind of amateur's curve cast to achieve the fabled drag-free drift. I was beginning to feel worthy of the rod. Maybe I would rise above my poor origins.

Sometime in the middle of the summer I was persuaded to go out at night, which was, they said, the only time to catch big trout on the Pere Marquette. My friend who had come up from Detroit to open the little shop obligingly sold me a dozen flies for night fishing. Any one of them would cover the palm of your hand and the hooks were so big they looked dangerous. I still hit myself in the head with my fly once or twice a day and I knew that if it happened with one of these beauties I would need to make a trip to the emergency room. But I was game.

And behold, I actually caught a fish that could be called "big" by the relaxed standards of the Pere Marquette. It would have been merely a "nice fish" west of the Mississippi, but here it was a little better than that. The fish ran off line and worked all over the pool I was fishing. He felt very strong in the darkness and he looked bigger than he was when I finally got him in the beam of my light. I felt like I had arrived.

So I took a trip north to visit the Two Hearted. Actually, if you want to fish the river that Nick Adams fished in the famous story, go to the Fox; Hemingway used the name of the other river for reasons that are obvious. But it was a sort of pilgrimage, this trip, and by the end of the summer, I felt I had earned it.

The fishing was slow, but I didn't really care. The countryside was magnificent, full of meaning beyond its undeniable beauty. I had a memorable three or four days, and thought once or twice about what a splendid gift the rod had been.

I had learned an awful lot in less than a year. Enough to make me a trout fisherman and give me a pastime that will last me, I trust, as long as I live. I would never say that I learned the best way. In fact, I would listen respectfully to anyone who wanted to say that I learned in the worst way. Books by themselves are not good teachers. And trial and error is a sure way to learn bad habits, which I did and am still having trouble with. But I was never going to learn unless I learned that way. And I still remember that summer when I would drive to the Pere Marquette on Fridays and take a little cabin by the river and fall asleep thinking of the next day's fishing. I learned more and caught less than I have most summers since then. There were times that still live vividly in my memory. The time I worked a rising fish through five fly changes before I got him to take. Another time when I stumbled on a great hatch of some kind of dark, late-season mayfly, tied on an Adams, and took my limit for the first time ever. My first look at a really big fish, a steelhead, late that fall, when the leaves had changed color and you could hear the occasional blast of a grouse hunter's shotgun off in the distance. I wouldn't have had any of that if it had not been for the rod, which is still my favorite among an accumulation of speedier cane models, graphites, and even boron/graphites. The rod is one of the few things I own that I am genuinely sentimental about and I wouldn't take anything for it. It was my teacher.

The Bonefish Flats

Charles F. Waterman

The Bonefish Flats

"THAT'S FRED!" I said, standing on a Bimini dock and watching a bonefish skiff idle toward wherever it would be tied up for the night.

He was tall, powerful, and assured, a big black man at the wheel of his specialized boat, casting platform up forward, shallow draft, pushpole lashed along the gunwale—a pushpole polished to a patina by powerful and knowing hands. The client, pinkish despite sun lotion and broad hat, was slumped comfortably in his chair with the self-satisfied look tourist anglers get as they approach a dock and a hotel bar after a good day.

"It's Fred all right," Debie said at my elbow. "Should we yell to him?"

We didn't yell and Fred continued on his way, the big outboard ticking along with the boat's gentle wake lapping the dock. Fred never noticed us and probably wouldn't have known us even if we'd called him by name. It had been a long time. We felt a little older and as if we'd had some special connection with Bahama bonefish all those years.

It was quite a distance from Bimini where we had met Fred, a gangling youngster, mostly legs, hands, and feet. It was over at Abaco Island, and the resort manager, as new as Fred in the bonefish business, had asked us to help show Fred how to guide fishermen. Fred knew about bonefish, and his people ate them. My wife Debie never really convinced him they were worth more as gamefish than as food.

Fred had white-eyed amazement for the snaking coils of fly line, and when he netted the first bonefish he'd seen taken on a fly his grin was enormous, although he was not quite sure then why bonefish shouldn't be caught some easier and more practical way. Seeing him in the cloth and skiff of a real professional reminded us that we'd been around bonefish for a long time.

Bonefishing comes to my memory in bits and pieces from the past, beginning some thirty years ago. I remember very little of the first one I caught on a fly, a fish that came the hard way in the Florida Keys after weeks of fruitless hunting and casting. "No guide," I'd said in the cocksure confidence of ignorance, so we fished for bones at the wrong time of year (winter) and lived in a little trailer. They just weren't on the flats at first, and we were not quite sure when we did see one at a distance. And then Debie caught some on a spinning rod and a little Wiggle Jig, and I, from some careless advice, used leader tippets that were too light and broke off several.

The only thing I remember about my first bonefish is that Debie scooped it into a net and said, *"There's* my Charley's bonefish." I recall no other time that she has ever said "my Charley" to my face, so it was a sort of emotional thing, though we wouldn't have mentioned it at the time.

As others have wanted to walk on the moon and some have wished to scale Everest, I wanted to catch a bonefish on a fly, an accomplishment I felt was a culmination of the entire art of fly-fishing.

I toyed with the thought in California as I cast for trout and bass. I read the tales of bonefishing, some of them so dramatized that the subject swam seventy miles an hour and was caught only on casts of more than one hundred feet. I read about reels that exploded from searing runs. The leading bonefish hero was Joe Brooks, who had developed fly-fishing for them and who moved to the Florida Keys to be with them.

It was not Brooks who cloaked the bonefish in wild hyperbole, though, nor was it Allen Corson, who had aided Brooks in his early fishing for them. It was the "general" writers who visited the scene and competed for attention with extravagant statements about the fastest fish and the supermen who caught them. Ted Williams of baseball fame was a favored subject because an author could start with a newsworthy celebrity and attach him to a famous fish with that mysterious tool, the saltwater fly rod.

And when I had gone to the Keys and to the Bahamas and to Cuba, I was as mesmerized with bonefish as ever—not for the drama the authors had set forth, but for completely different reasons tied to the living saltwater flats, the shimmering, flowing world of the bonefish itself. Then I realized that although I might not want to spend a lifetime at bonefishing, the bonefish excited me more than the giant tarpon, the big brown trout rising for a minute fly, or even the Atlantic salmon turning to take something representing nothing he had ever before seen or wanted. So bonefishing is recalled in bits and pieces with little continuity, but bits and pieces that are completely unforgettable and never fading at all.

At Isle of Pines, south of Cuba, before Fidel Castro was even a public figure, we left the main island in a little wooden skiff to fish for bonefish, and we understood little of where we were going—only that Isle of Pines had many bonefish. The resort manager was away, and our guide, a calm youth with little to say, was from Grand Cayman. The motor was seven and one-half horsepower and there was a spare of the same size on the deck at our guide's feet.

The wind was high and tore water from the wave crests as we left a river mouth and moved out to sea, alternately facing a bright sky and walls of blue-green water, while the guide bailed steadily and cheerfully. When Ted Smallwood croaked a question as to where the hell we were going, the guide pointed straight ahead into the shoulder of an enormous wave and said, "To the island, sir."

Waters Swift and Still

We saw it a little later, a barely visible, darker streak where corrugated blue sea and blank blue sky met, and when we had reached it, a little blob of land surrounded by wide flats, we were uncomfortable because we knew that eventually we would have to return to the river through those fearsome seas.

But the seas were temporarily behind us when we arrived, and the great flat glittered with patches of moving fish, their various wake patterns catching the sun as they wheeled, settled, moved again, foraging on the fertile bottom. The guide applied his pole gently and removed his polarized glasses to read the surface rather than the fish themselves. He mentally discarded shark or barracuda wakes, even though the runout water was rather deep for them to show fins or tails, and he silently pointed to a little curl of movement only fifty feet away. It was a small bonefish, and Ted caught it after it had made a short run.

There were other small bonefish and a tarpon that boomed upward from a blue hole, but Ted was thinking of the big Keys bones and he tightened his drag to humiliate a small bonefish. He spoke disparagingly of Cuban bones, and the guide listened with a polite smile. Then he paused in his poling and said to Ted:

"*Big bone fish.*"

He said it in three distinctly separate words, and Ted cast ahead of a jutting fin and tail. There was a great swirl and the leader snapped. The guide's facial expression never changed, and I can still see the big fin and tail and its background of the enormous flat with the rollers far out past its edge. It was only two hours or so before the feeding fish left the shallows; the tide rose and the guide nosed the boat back toward the waves and toward Isle of Pines, a faint, ragged line on the horizon, visible only from the wave crests.

The Bonefish Flats

Bonefish are in the back of my mind so often when I cast for other species that I have repeatedly sought them under poor conditions, often with little preparation and no advance arrangements. Bonefish require preparation and advance arrangements.

There are flats at Cozumel, off Yucatán, flats that often swarm with bonefish, and there are also lagoons, sometimes with bonefish in deeper water. But my first Cozumel bonefishing trip was impromptu. I had come for some other fishing with anglers who lacked the bonefish passion, but I learned there was a man at the hotel who could guide me. The quest for bonefish often evaporates into strange journeys.

The man at the hotel had a Spanish nickname that meant "Snapper," and he had but a few words of English. He was red-haired and blocky, and he had an assistant who was dark, slim, silent, and youthful. Snapper was part of the hotel's white-jacketed staff, and he had to get permission from the manager before he could take me fishing the next morning. I watched him follow the manager at a discreet distance for more than half an hour, the propitious time for the request finally arriving, and the manager—plump stereotype of the Mexican businessman—said he could have the day off.

In early morning I found Snapper's boat pitching restlessly at the little hotel pier. It was no bonefish skiff. It had the lines of a small sailboat, and it was powered by an outboard. We went up along the coast for a long while, the Cozumel shore, like many tropical coasts, always intriguing to a man raised in Kansas—intriguing, wild, and foreign with its palms, mangroves, and white line of surf. There was a formation of flamingos, pleasantly grotesque birds, in distant silhouette, like a design in straight lines by some primitive artist.

We entered the first lagoon, and unprepared for such small bonefish, I took a scurrying school for mullet. Then I found the deep keel of the boat would not travel the lagoon's shallows and I began wading while my guide and his aide watched in bored half-interest. I hooked a small bone, and when the hook came out I could almost feel Snapper's resignation. He had done his share for me and now it was his turn to fish.

Snapper stood on the stern seat of his boat, bare feet planted solidly, his handline coiled neatly and automatically in his left hand, and he measured the distance to an angelfish undulating slowly across the flat. He whirled his baited hook above his head, and it arched slightly to splat softly ahead of the target. A moment later Snapper brought the fish in and hurried to rebait for a small shark.

I stood in knee-deep water and marl, the forgotten client, and watched the hotel worker, menial tasks of the resort inn forgotten, silhouetted confidently against a gathering storm and throwing his baits to anything that crossed the flat with almost a hundred-percent success.

The tide was lower when we left the flat, and when we shoved the awkward boat back through the little lagoon inlet we left a groove as the keel gouged the bottom. It was hard, grunting work. I suspected that the silent assistant (mate?) was not pushing his weight, but my fierce glare met a manufactured grimace of effort.

The carefully prepared hotel lunch had been left at the desk, but Snapper cheerfully produced three bananas and the threatening storm arrived in thunder and great stinging drops of horizontal rain. The choppy inshore waves pitched the little boat and the nearby shoreline dimmed. There, with the motor buzzing importantly, Snapper cleaned his catch. And even in the rain I felt my view darkened. Above me were two frigate birds, hovering no more than five feet up. Their great wings spread so far that I shrank, some throwback to fear of some colossal prehistoric birds of prey. But they had somehow sensed the scraps from Snapper's fish cleaning.

There was a break in the storm and the wind changed. Snapper rigged what appeared to be a primitive mast and sail but he did it with sleight-of-hand and I felt it gather the wind and strain for the hotel miles down the coast.

Snapper stood with his feet widespread and looked down at me with a tight smile of pride, peering over his wet barrel chest.

"Me, sailor!" he snapped. "Yucatán!" Seamen have that pride the world over.

Then the storm struck again, and when we finally saw the rain-shrouded hotel and its whipping palms the boat had been bailed constantly. Snapper's assistant seized the pier as we came alongside, and as I walked soggily into the lobby I met an acquaintance who had caught three sailfish that morning. He carried a drink in his hand. "How was bonefishing?" he asked.

What would you have answered?

Cozumel has wonderful bonefishing. I just missed it.

For a century, sportsmen have discovered bonefish on their own. It is the famous fishermen or the writers whose discoveries are recorded, and sometimes their reports ignore the findings of others who have gone long before them.

When Dr. James Henshall made his discovery of the bonefish so many years ago, that normally reliable authority became wildly inaccurate. In his work on the subject he states that the bonefish jumps furiously, but unlike other confused students he had not mixed up the bonefish and the ladyfish. He says that the ladyfish jumps too.

And Zane Grey and his brother went to the Florida Keys in 1919 to investigate the mystery fish, and with the pride of other experienced anglers they decided to do it without the aid of local guides. Grey's story of the fiasco was rather pompous comedy to later bonefishermen. The Greys assumed a super fish was best handled with heavy tackle. But the bonefish, as later anglers learned, must be fished with finesse rather than power. It would be incredible to the Greys that other generations of anglers have caught big bonefish with four-pound-test line and with fly equipment commonly used for brook trout.

There are other places where the bonefish are more plentiful and more easily caught, but it was in the Florida Keys that they first became famous and the Keys fish remain among the largest and most difficult to catch. Casters who have sought them around the world and have caught a dozen or more in a day may still return to the Keys with as much anticipation as ever. There is special appeal to fish that live with man, listen to his propellers, and see his airplanes. Some of the greatest of the bonefish anglers do it within view of Miami Beach's skyline. It is much like the big bonefish that idle among the swimmers on a Bermuda beach, and the appeal of lonely waters seldom fished is offset by the knowledge that the fish pursued has been sought by a hundred good fishermen and has grown big and wise in frustrating them.

The Keys themselves have their own subtropical appeal, even though traffic roars on the Keys Highway less than a mile away and the clank of drag lines in tortured sand and coral is still heard.

There is the Keys community of wildlife, the cormorants that skim the flats at low tide, their routes marked by the wakes of small fish that have been startled by their ominous shadows, and the patient herons along the shore. At morning and evening, especially, there is the eerie, hooting *coo* of the white-crowned fruit pigeon somewhere in the mangroves, often seen singly or in little flocks trading between the islands.

On the ocean side of the upper Keys there is the offshore parade of freighters and gleaming yachts following the sea lane, some days a little hazy in outline while on other days brilliantly displayed by bright sun against blue sky and ocean.

Then, too, there is the study of fish and their movements. They grow familiar, even with respect to the individual fish or individual schools. Best of all is to find the fish by design rather than accident.

On my ocean-side flat the fishing is best at low tide, whether rising or falling, and for some reason the fish's movement is always predominantly northeastward when they are traveling. Of course, they must return southwestward in deeper water, for I am sure most of them are the same fish day after day—fish that know the coast and patrol the same feeding areas when time, tide, and temperature are right.

The classic time is during midday if there is a low tide then, and if the sun is bright the hunt is simpler. I use the wreck as a gauge. The wreck has been there for a long time, and when I first saw it more than twenty-five years ago there was much more of it lodged on the shallow reef at the edge of my flat.

Even then it had been there for a long time, and I think I once heard how it got there, but it didn't seem important then and I have forgotten. Now it is gradually disappearing into the bottom. It never had been a very large craft and now it is noticeable only at low tide with an occasional cormorant drying its wings on it. At high tide there may be a barracuda lying in ambush there, and nearly always there are a few small mangrove snappers willing to come out of hiding for a bonefish fly in a single, darting foray. After that they will ignore it.

But when the wreck is showing plainly I pole the skiff in from deeper water, where my propeller has fouled irritatingly in seaweed, and I push in close to the little point at one end of the flat. The flat must narrow to the point, and any bonefish moving up the coast are likely to pass around it close to shore, a natural funnel. If I sight several fish I get out and wade, leaving the skiff anchored far enough out that it won't be left aground as the tide recedes.

When most of the flat is no more than eight or ten inches deep, I watch for tailers near the shore as well as traveling fish farther out. In bright sun the tails are always larger than I expect, quivering and waving as their owners pursue tidbits on the bottom. I cannot approach a tailer calmly and logically, so I nearly always misjudge the distance. Too much line and I lay the leader across it; too short a cast and the fly is too far away for it to see. But if the fly alights neatly within a foot or so of the fish's nose, the gleaming tail may freeze instantly and for a long moment the fish is immobilized, like a dog on point. Then if the tail moves quickly and the fish noses down on the little fly, there is the most important instant of all, for I must wait for some tiny signal before setting the hook—a twitch of the leader or a gentle tug, often imagined before it comes.

Where the water is a little deeper, somewhat farther from shore, the search is more complicated. If I am drifting in the boat, I have the advantage of height and I pay special attention to the lighter areas of the blotchy bottom, for the fish are hard to see over dark grass patches. Then there is the "nervous water," not exactly a wake, but a surface disturbance of some sort made by the fish, often seen from a long way off on a windless midday, and with practice it can be interpreted—sometimes it is a busy school of tiny fish and sometimes it is made by a shark or a barracuda. But it can be a single bonefish or a school of them.

As I drift silently on a breezy day my eyes tire from constant attention to the shifting, writhing, distorted view of the bottom passing beneath me. If I am alone I tend to repeat an inane jingle that came to me on some long-ago tide:

Oh the bonefish lives in a wiggly world, in a wiggly world lives he,
He dines upon crab and very small shrimp and he cares not for you and me.

I am a little shocked that prolonged concentration upon a bonefish flat could lead me to such vapid doggerel, but the thing comes back regularly and I have never thought of further rhyme to go with it.

The bottom slides past with its picturesque distortions of coral and its spiny, black clumps of sea urchins. Trunkfish move stiffly away and small sharks are likely to stare myopically at the boat for some time and then flush in panic. A thousand times I have sighted a stationary barracuda of just the right size at just the right angle and identified it as a bonefish, even to the point of casting to it. But on a slow day I might try it even if I knew what it was.

A wader can approach much closer to a fish in most cases, but many a bonefish has been caught after it has studied the boat and its occupants and even after it has turned aside to let it pass. Especially from a school there is the chance that a fish reluctant to break formation might nevertheless dart a few inches to one side to scoop up the fly.

In the deeper water, the fish are likely to be traveling, and placing a fly the right distance ahead so that it will sink to the exact spot at the right time through a foot or more of depth becomes a problem of trajectory. Most flies are weighted to match the depth, for the bonefish is a bottom feeder first and foremost, and seldom moves upward to take a fly.

In summer there are times when the shallow flats are too warm at midday, and if there is to be a low tide in the evening, it is the best time to look for tailers. My largest fish have been taken and lost then, their broad tails glistening near the shore, where barnacles snap and crackle like breakfast cereals when exposed to the air. If I wade only an easy cast from shore I may see a fish coming a long way off, its tail and fins appearing and disappearing again as it investigates the thousand things a bonefish must examine.

That was how I watched the really big bonefish, and I actually stood amid a school of tailing lesser ones as I saw him coming. For some reason the usually receptive evening feeders had become finicky, not flushing badly but apparently uninterested in dabs of hair and feather. When I saw the big bonefish coming I was actually within casting range of several smaller fish that showed intermittently, out of sight part of the time since the water was deep enough to cover them unless they tipped up.

The sun was just down and most of the white ibis and egrets had gathered and gone to their roosts, tinted by the last rays. The cooling flat had taken on the mystery of evening with the bottom no longer visible. I was more than two hundred yards inland from the little reef where the old wreck lies, and farther out is such an entrapment of seaweed and sea fans that a bonefish running that far before he begins to circle under pressure has generally made his escape.

When the big fish had worked its way along the shore until it was only a long cast away, it moved into slightly deeper water and disappeared momentarily. Then I saw a fin and tail briefly and made a cast to it, but as the leader straightened and the floating line roped up from where it had been coiled in the water at my knee, I knew it was not the big bonefish. It was a poor cast, too long, and the leader fell across the big fish's back. It started briefly, never flushed, but moved away slowly, abandoning that immediate feeding area.

There was some sort of commotion then in almost the same spot, sensed as much as seen, and I cast once more, the little pink-and-tan fly making its tiny *plip* above the disturbance. It sank a foot or so toward the bottom, and I began the jerky, inching retrieve so fondly thought to represent frightened crabs, shrimps, and minnows. The fly stopped.

It has stopped thousands of times when it has struck coral, grass, or stone, but I flipped the rod tip upward and sideways to strike as I have those thousands of times. There was a slow, surly movement. This time there was no boiling swirl and no singing rush for deep water with the reel crying and the line leaving a little surface geyser as it goes. This time the fish simply swam away slowly and there were sullen tugs as he shook his head over something unsatisfactory. Then he ran, a great boil marking his departure point, and I put the rod tip up and breathlessly watched my running line whip through my fingers and the guides, that moment of truth when the fish either gets on the reel or something tangles and snaps.

The line reached the reel and it started smoothly and buzzed steadily while I made frantic plans. *When the fish has gone two hundred yards*, I thought, *I'll try to slow it with added tension.* I had never had a fish that felt like this one and I had no doubt it could go three hundred yards or more, well out into the deeper water with its clutching growth.

But the plans were never executed. It slashed for seventy-five yards and simply stopped. The fish was lost. It did not know where deep water lay, obviously out of its home territory and unfamiliar with the surroundings. It came almost directly toward me and I cranked wildly in despair. But again I had a tight line, the backing on the reel, and the fish only thirty yards away. It roared off in a new direction and the reel paid out evenly, and then in uncertain spurts with short pauses. My fish was hopelessly confused.

It was dark when I subdued it after a dozen short dashes instead of the traditional runs. I drew it against my leg, my hand under its broad belly, and it felt hard and heavy. I worked the little fly out of its jaw and released it. Then I waded off toward the boat at anchor over near the wreck. As I walked, another fish flushed at my feet and I started with the apprehension almost all men feel in darkness.

The next day I stood in a tackle shop and appraised a mounted specimen that had won a tournament. *Mine was bigger than that*, I thought.

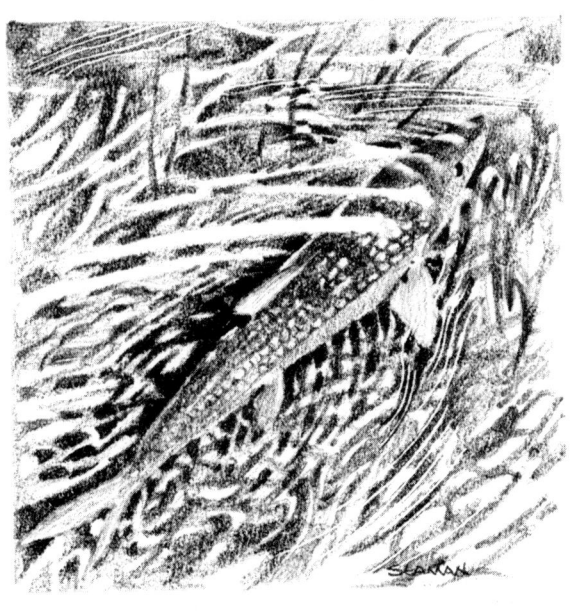

Epilogue
David Seybold

ON AN early-spring day, when the woods still held snow and streams and brooks ran full with snowmelt, a boy and his father were fly-fishing for brook trout on a mountain tarn in New England. It was a warm, sunny day without any wind, and the surface of the small pond was still and reflected the surrounding pine forest and large cumulus clouds that drifted overhead.

They had launched their canoe early, when the sun was not high enough to warm them, and the father had caught a fat, smelt-filled brook trout right off. But the boy, who had just begun fly-fishing, had been unsuccessful in getting anything to take his streamer.

After a few hours had passed without another trout being caught, the boy momentarily resigned himself to catching nothing. He sat in the bow with his back to his father and closed his eyes and listened to his father's fly-casting.

His father did not say anything to him. He did not have to. The boy had fished the streamer well and he knew that the boy would not give up, that he would keep trying until he succeeded. The boy had a lot of his grandfather in him. And it made the man think about the hundreds of hours he and his father had spent fishing and how his father would never give up when trout were rising all around them and they could not catch any. The boy has that same determination, his father thought. He has it in him to never give up.

For now, though, the boy was content to rest and listen. Hearing a person, especially his father, fly-cast, was almost as enjoyable as actually doing it. So he sat with his eyes closed and the sun warm on his skin and the sound of his father's fly-casting soothing his taut senses.

He could hear his father pick the fly line off the water, hear the rod and line reach back beyond the canoe and over the surface of the pond. A *whish-whish* sound filled the air as his father began false-casting. They were quick casts that required little effort. But then the sound became lower and more laborious, a *whoosh-whoosh* sound, as the length of line and pressure on the rod increased. In his mind, the boy could see perfectly the slender bamboo rod fully loaded, with line arching back then thrusting forward, the line's long loop gracefully uncurling before the streamer lit on the surface.

Then came a long silence as the boy's father waited for the streamer to sink. And then, almost abruptly, because there was no warning, came the sound of the fly line being stripped in. The boy always tried to place the sound that the line made when it was being pulled through the guides. It sounded like something else, something he knew very well. But he could never place it, and he always wondered.

The boy opened his eyes and saw a brace of wood ducks fly low over the pond and land on the far shore. He knew his father would stop fishing and watch the ducks. They were his father's favorite kind, especially the males.

When his father resumed casting and stripping in, the boy thought he had had enough of a rest. He was ready to try again, finally to catch his first trout on a fly. And as he started to false-cast, his father paused and listened and smiled.

Ten, fifteen, twenty, twenty-five feet and the boy let his fly line and streamer land and sink. Again and again he cast and retrieved. And again and again nothing happened. He would have welcomed a snag, anything to make his rod bend and spirits rise.

Just as he completed another cast, his father hooked a trout and he turned to watch, letting his line and streamer slowly sink. His father played the trout for several minutes before it finally came to net. It was another beautiful, fat brook trout, and they both admired it as the boy's father held it just under the surface, patiently waiting for it to revive and swim away.

The boy turned back to his line, more determined than ever to catch a trout. The line had sunk very deep and he stripped it in faster than normal so he could start casting again.

Then it happened. It was as though the streamer had hooked onto a cement wall. The rod bent low and the line angled deep. The tip of the rod pulsated up and down, and the boy could feel the line that lay in loose coils on the bottom of the canoe slip under his index finger.

He could not believe it, and when the line he had stripped in was all out again and the reel began to pay out more, he could no longer contain himself and he shouted: "I have one! I have one! I have a *trout!*"

The boy held the rod with both hands and let the line come off the reel and run between his index finger and the cork handle. It was a big trout, that much the boy was certain of, and he wanted to catch it more than anything in the world.

"How long should I let him run?" asked the boy. "He already has half the line out."

"Don't worry about that now," his father finally said. "You just keep pressure on him, like you're doing. He'll get tired pretty soon. Make him work for every inch he gets."

The boy's father was keeping his eye on the angle of the line. And when it started to cut deeper into the water, he knew the trout was heading down. He leaned forward, then, and spoke to the boy in a calm and reassuring voice.

"Try to keep him from going to the bottom. He's going to try to wrap the leader around a rock or stump and break off. See if you can bring him up a little bit at a time. Raise the rod slowly and then lower it while you strip in the slack line."

The boy listened, but instinct more than anything accounted for following his father's instructions. Slowly the trout began to come up, and the boy's father, though worried and nervous, looked on with pride. He's a natural fly fisherman, he thought. A real natural.

Waters Swift and Still

When the trout was close to the canoe, the father slipped the net into the water and told the boy to swing his rod toward the stern. Then they saw the trout five feet away and a yard down. And just then the trout saw the hull of the canoe and the net and made a frantic attempt to escape. But it was too little too late, and when the trout made another run, the boy handled the rod and line perfectly.

At last it was over and both father and son looked into the water where the fifteen-inch trout lay in the mesh of the net. The father swung the net out of the water and handed it to his son.

The boy stared down at the brook trout. Its body was speckled and silky, and it shone through the mesh. Then the boy watched it shake and quiver, saw that it was still struggling to be free.

"Will it live if I put it back?" he asked.

The boy's father was stunned at the question. Seeing his son hold his first trout had reminded him of when he had caught his first trout. That was many years ago, and he remembered how he had dragged it around for an entire afternoon, showing it off to friends and neighbors.

"Yes. He's in good shape. But are you sure you want to? *He is your first trout.*"

"Yes, he's too beautiful to die," said the boy.

Then the boy reached into the net and cleared the hook and leader from the trout and lowered the net back into the water. He let the net fall away so that he held the trout with one hand. And when the trout's gills began to beat faster and its tail worked back and forth steadily, he let go and watched it move away. At first the trout was uncertain and moved slowly, but then it gained confidence in its freedom and darted suddenly out of sight.

It was at that moment, that instant when the trout disappeared from both the boy's and the father's view, that the father heard his son say something he would never forget.

"Thank you," said the boy. "Thank you very much. I hope you live forever."

About the Authors

NELSON BRYANT ("Catch and Release and Other Things"), outdoor editor of *The New York Times*, has contributed numerous stories and articles about fishing and hunting to the country's leading outdoor magazines.

CHARLES GAINES ("Home Waters") is a novelist whose books include *Pumping Iron* and *Dangler*.

ART LEE ("The Way of Consolation") is a freelance writer and the northeast field editor for *Fly Fisherman* magazine. His articles have appeared in *Sports Illustrated, Sports Afield, National Geographic, Fly Fisherman,* and other magazines.

NICK LYONS ("City Angler") is the author of *Bright Rivers, Fishing Widows,* and *The Seasonable Angler.* He also publishes angling books under the name Nick Lyons Books.

JOHN MERWIN ("Stillwaters Run Deep") is the editor and publisher of *Rod and Reel* magazine, and was editor of the book *Stillwater Trout.*

GEOFFREY NORMAN ("Just a Rod Away") is a columnist for *Esquire* magazine. His first novel is scheduled for publication in the spring of 1982.

JOHN RANDOLPH ("Notes on Alaska") is managing editor of *Fly Fisherman* magazine, a newspaper columnist, and the author of numerous articles for outdoor magazines.

STEVE RAYMOND ("October: A Northwest Idyll"), a newspaper editor by trade, is the author of the prize-winning book *Kamloops* and past editor of *The Fly Fisher,* the quarterly publication of the Federation of Fly Fishermen.

Waters Swift and Still

ERNEST SCHWIEBERT ("Some Reflections on Failure") is widely recognized as a leading fly-fishing authority and writer. His books include *Matching the Hatch, Nymphs, Trout,* and *Death of a Riverkeeper.*

ROBERT TRAVER ("Gamboling at Frenchman's") is the author of *Trout Madness* and *Trout Magic,* as well as numerous other books and stories about fly-fishing for trout. He also is the author of the best-selling novel *Anatomy of a Murder.*

CHARLES F. WATERMAN ("The Bonefish Flats") has been called the Dean of Outdoor Writers. His numerous books include many on fishing, and he contributes regularly to the outdoor press. Among his latest books is *A History of Angling.*

LEE WULFF ("Fly-Fishing: An Angler's Perspective") is one of the best-known anglers of our time. His television series *The American Sportsman* brought angling into the homes of thousands of Americans. His book *The Atlantic Salmon* is considered a classic work on salmon fishing.

DAVID SEYBOLD, co-editor of this book, is a freelance writer and editor with an avid interest in all things related to angling. His partner in the gathering of this new garland of fishing stories is also a freelance writer and editor, CRAIG WOODS, author of *The Fly Fisherman's Streamside Handbook.*